This book belongs to:

_____

Brighter Child®
Carson-Dellosa Publishing LLC
PO Box 35665
Greensboro, NC 27425 USA

© 2019 Carson-Dellosa Publishing LLC. Except as permitted under the United States Copyright Act, no part of this publication may be reproduced, stored, or distributed in any form or by any means (mechanically, electronically, recording, etc.) without the prior written consent of Carson-Dellosa Publishing LLC. Brighter Child® is an imprint of Carson-Dellosa Publishing LLC.

Printed in the USA • All rights reserved.   ISBN 978-1-4838-5404-5
01-309187784

AN INTRODUCTION TO COMIC BOOK DESIGN

"HELLO, COMIC CREATOR! MY NAME IS **SKETCH**, AND I CAN'T WAIT TO DRAW SOME COMICS WITH YOU."

"LET'S START BY TALKING ABOUT STORIES."

THE PARTS OF A STORY

IN THE BEGINNING, THE HERO AND LOCATION ARE INTRODUCED.

THE HERO ENCOUNTERS A CONFLICT. THE CONFLICT IS A PROBLEM THAT THE HERO MUST DEAL WITH TO MOVE FURTHER ALONG IN THE STORY.

THE HERO OFTEN HAS AN "AH-HA MOMENT" AND GAINS THE INFORMATION OR ABILITY NEEDED TO SOLVE THE CONFLICT.

THE HERO SOLVES THE CONFLICT AT THE END OF THE STORY.

ALL ABOUT CHARACTERS

WHAT ARE THE STRENGTHS THAT MAKE YOUR HERO SPECIAL?

WEAKNESSES ARE IMPORTANT, TOO. THEY KEEP YOUR HERO INTERESTING.

YOUR HERO COULD HAVE SUPER STRENGTH, BUT UNFORTUNATELY IS ALSO EXTREMELY CLUMSY. LOOK AT THESE IDEAS.

STRENGTHS	
NIGHT VISION	SUPER STRENGTH
KINDNESS	INVISIBILITY
FLYING	GENIUS
HEALING	
SUPER SPEED	BRAVERY
TIME TRAVEL	SEE THE FUTURE
CURIOSITY	TALK TO ANIMALS

WEAKNESSES	
CLUMSY	CATCHES ON FIRE
ALWAYS LATE	LOVES CHOCOLATE
SLOW HEALING	GETS LOST
FEAR OF LOUD NOISES	GETS TIRED
GIVES OFF RADIATION	SUPER SLOW
CAN'T SWIM	FEAR OF ANIMALS

A HERO NEEDS A SUPPORTING CAST OF CHARACTERS TO HELP MOVE THE STORY FORWARD. LOOK AT THESE IDEAS.

SIDEKICK

THE BEST FRIEND WHO YOUR HERO WILL PROTECT AT ALL COSTS

MENTOR

A KNOWLEDGEABLE CHARACTER WHO GUIDES YOUR HERO

VILLAIN

YOUR HERO'S ENEMY

THE NUTS AND BOLTS OF CHARACTER CREATION!

"LET'S CREATE THE **COSTUME ELEMENTS** FOR YOUR HERO."

"THESE EXAMPLES WILL HELP GET YOUR HERO STARTED!"

HEADGEAR	ACCESSORIES
FOOTWEAR	GLOVES

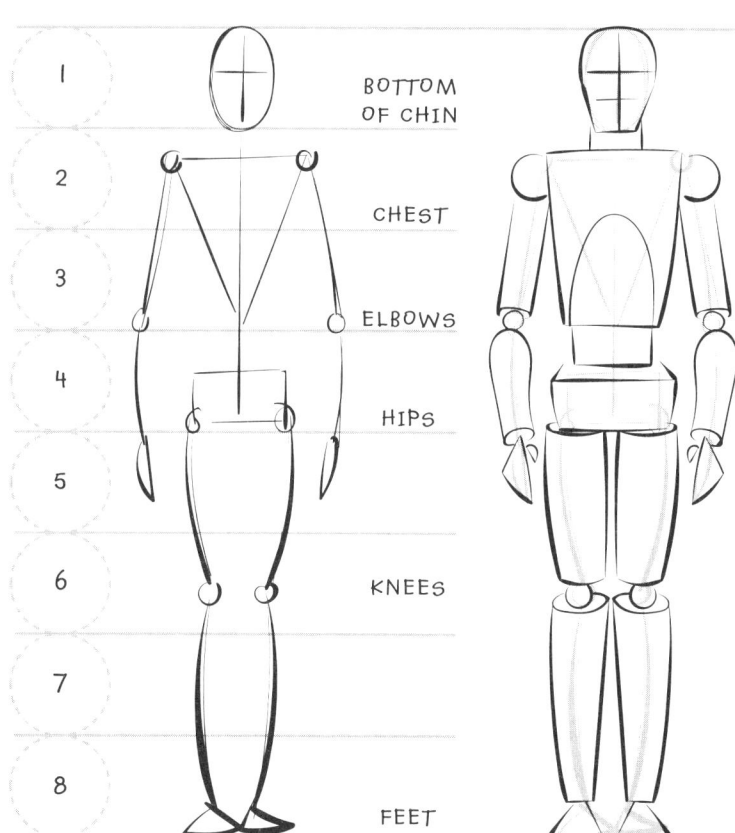

"START WITH A STICK FIGURE WHEN YOU BEGIN TO DRAW YOUR CHARACTER."

"THEN, DRAW BASIC SHAPES OVER THE STICK FIGURE."

"TO DRAW A REALISTIC FIGURE, THE AVERAGE HEIGHT IS SEVEN AND A HALF TO EIGHT HEADS TALL."

1 — BOTTOM OF CHIN
2 — CHEST
3 — ELBOWS
4 — HIPS
5
6 — KNEES
7
8 — FEET

"KEEP IN MIND THAT THE ELBOWS LINE UP WITH THE WAIST AND THE WRISTS LINE UP WITH THE HIPS."

PLAYING EVERY ANGLE!

THINK ABOUT WHAT CAMERA ANGLE WILL BEST TELL YOUR STORY IN EACH PANEL. HERE ARE SOME OPTIONS TO TRY.

BIRD'S-EYE VIEW

PANEL VIEWED FROM ABOVE LOOKING DOWN ON THE SCENE

WORM'S-EYE VIEW

PANEL VIEWED FROM BELOW LOOKING UP AT THE SCENE

CLOSE-UP

PANEL ZOOMED IN VERY TIGHT TO FOCUS ON THE CHARACTER OR AN OBJECT

LONG SHOT

PANEL VIEWED FROM A LONG DISTANCE TO SHOW WHERE THE SCENE IS TAKING PLACE

WRITING A SCRIPT

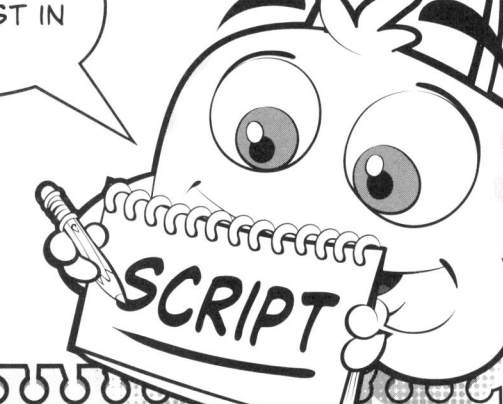

"IT IS ALWAYS BEST TO WRITE OUT YOUR STORY FIRST IN SCRIPT FORM."

"THIS WILL MAKE IT EASIER TO PLAN OUT YOUR PANELS AND TO LEAVE ENOUGH SPACE FOR YOUR WORD BALLOONS."

BASIC SCRIPT EXAMPLE

DESCRIBE WHAT HAPPENS IN EACH PANEL. BELOW THE PANEL DESCRIPTION, WRITE THE NAMES OF CHARACTERS THAT SPEAK FOLLOWED BY WHAT THEY SAY.

PANEL 1: A kid is playing fetch with a dog on the beach in the sun and sand. The kid throws the ball as the dog chases it.

Kid: Get it, boy!
Dog: Woof! Woof!

PANEL 2: The dog chases after the ball and a crab snatches it.
Dog: Woof?
Sound Effect: Snap!

FOLLOW THE SCRIPT ABOVE TO DRAW YOUR PANELS.

PANEL 1

PANEL 2

MAKE SURE TO LEAVE SPACE FOR WORD BALLOONS AND SOUND EFFECTS.

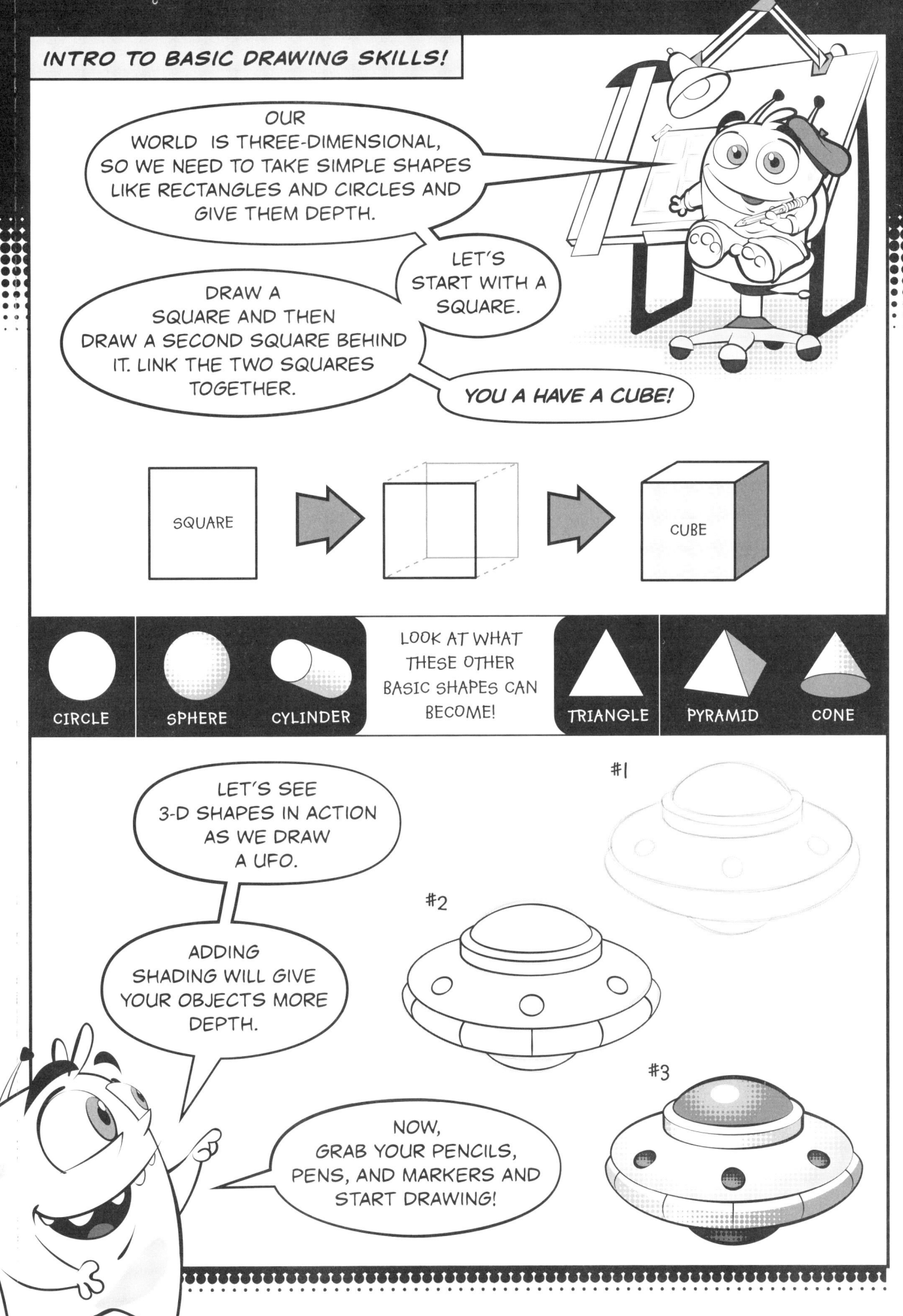

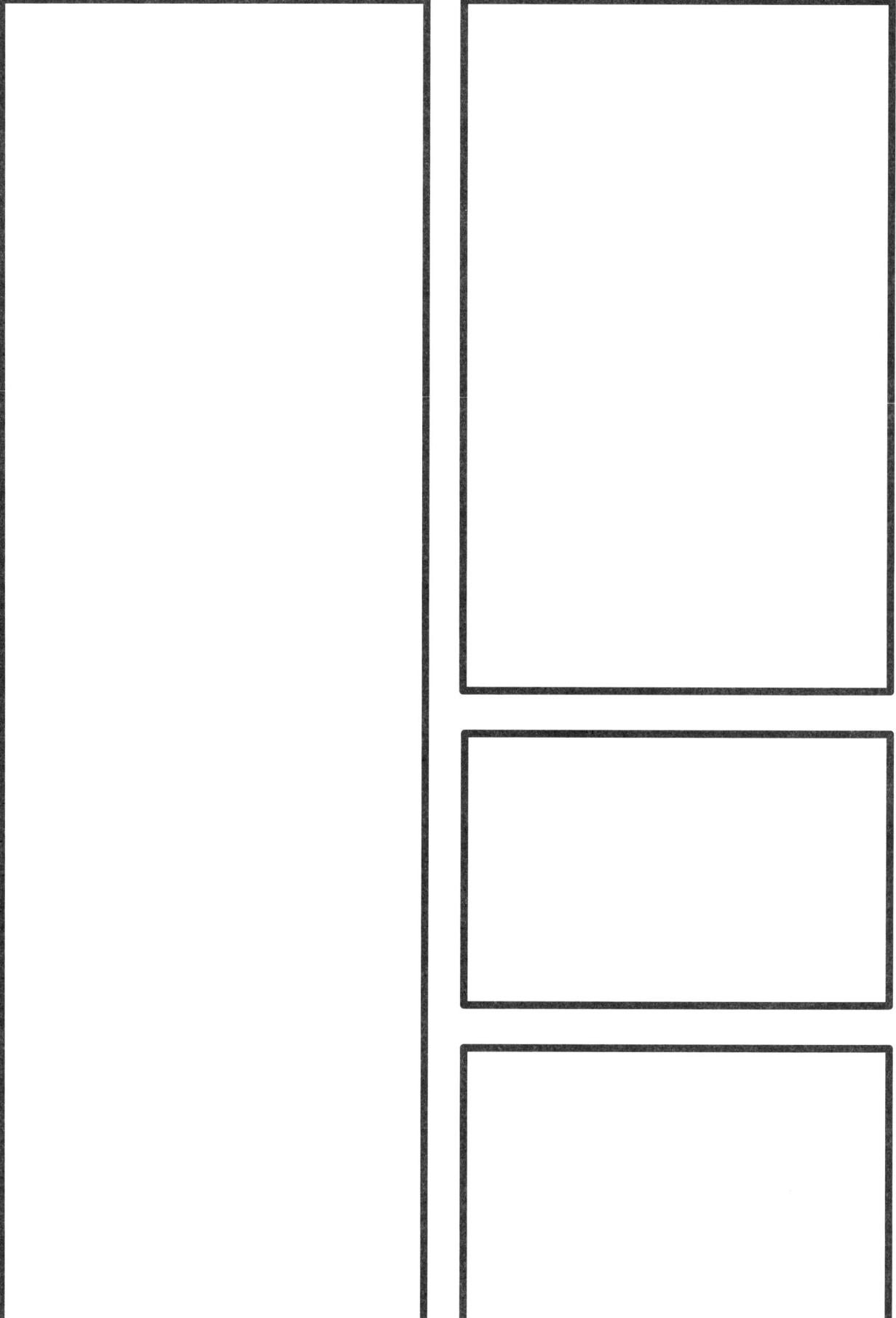

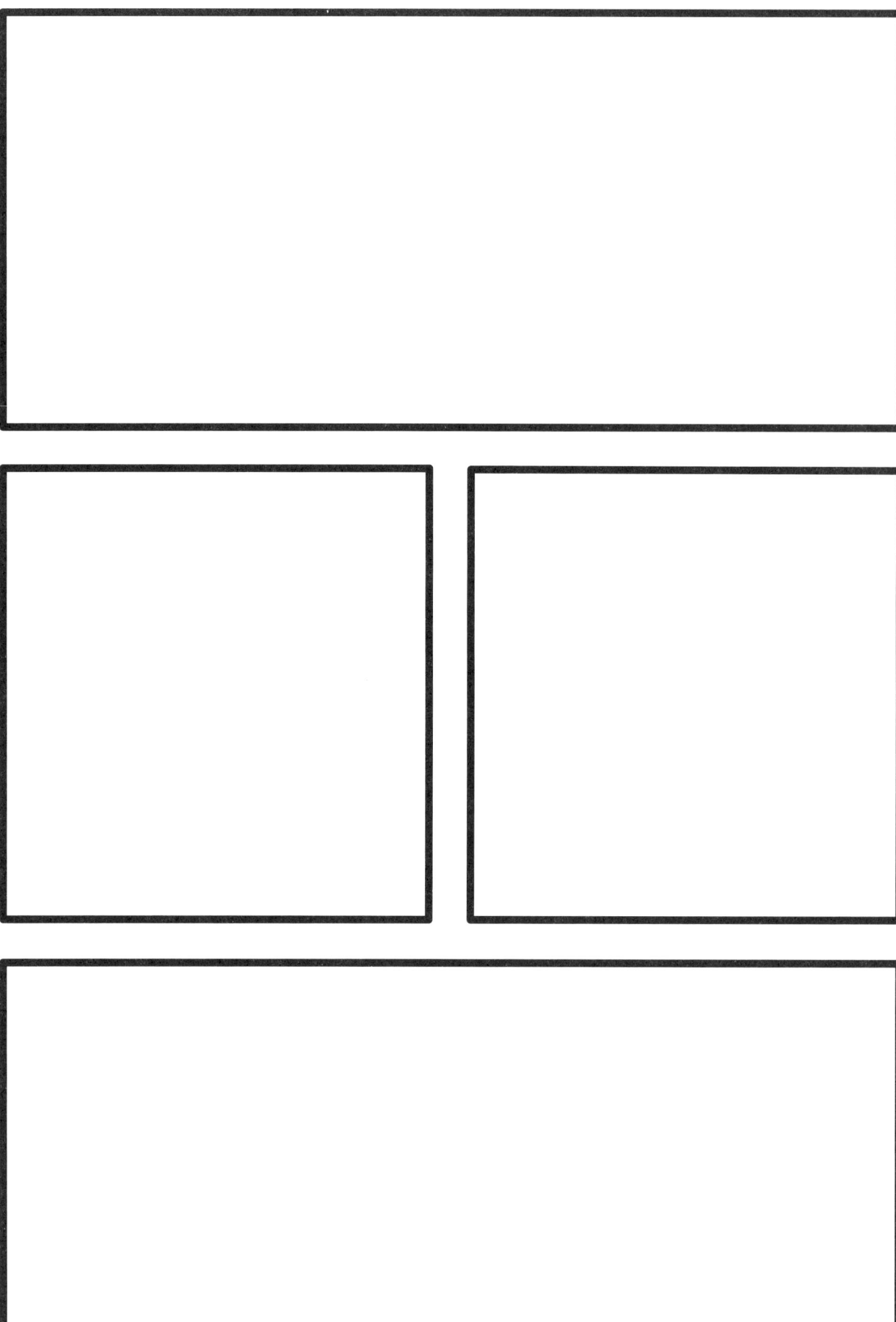

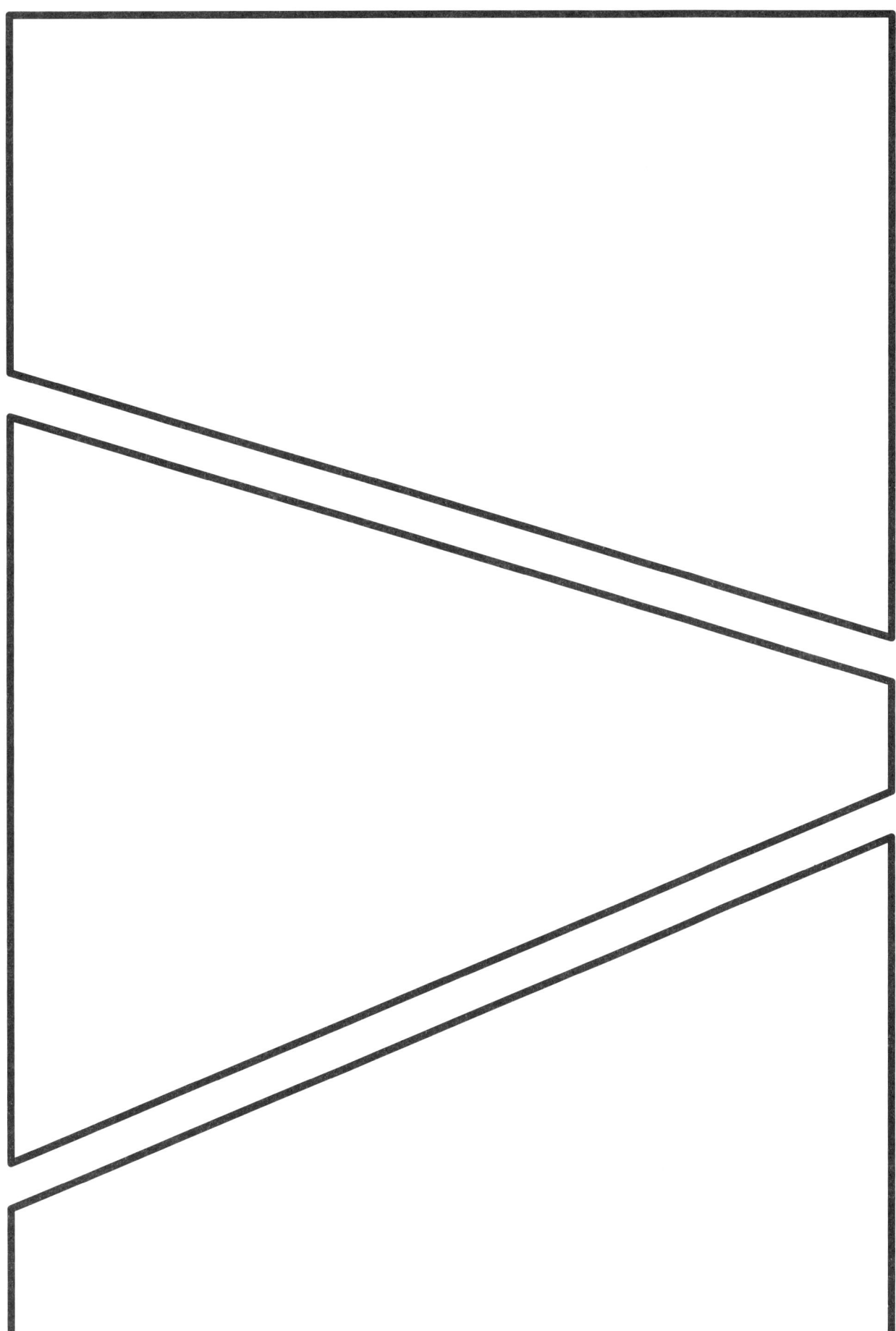

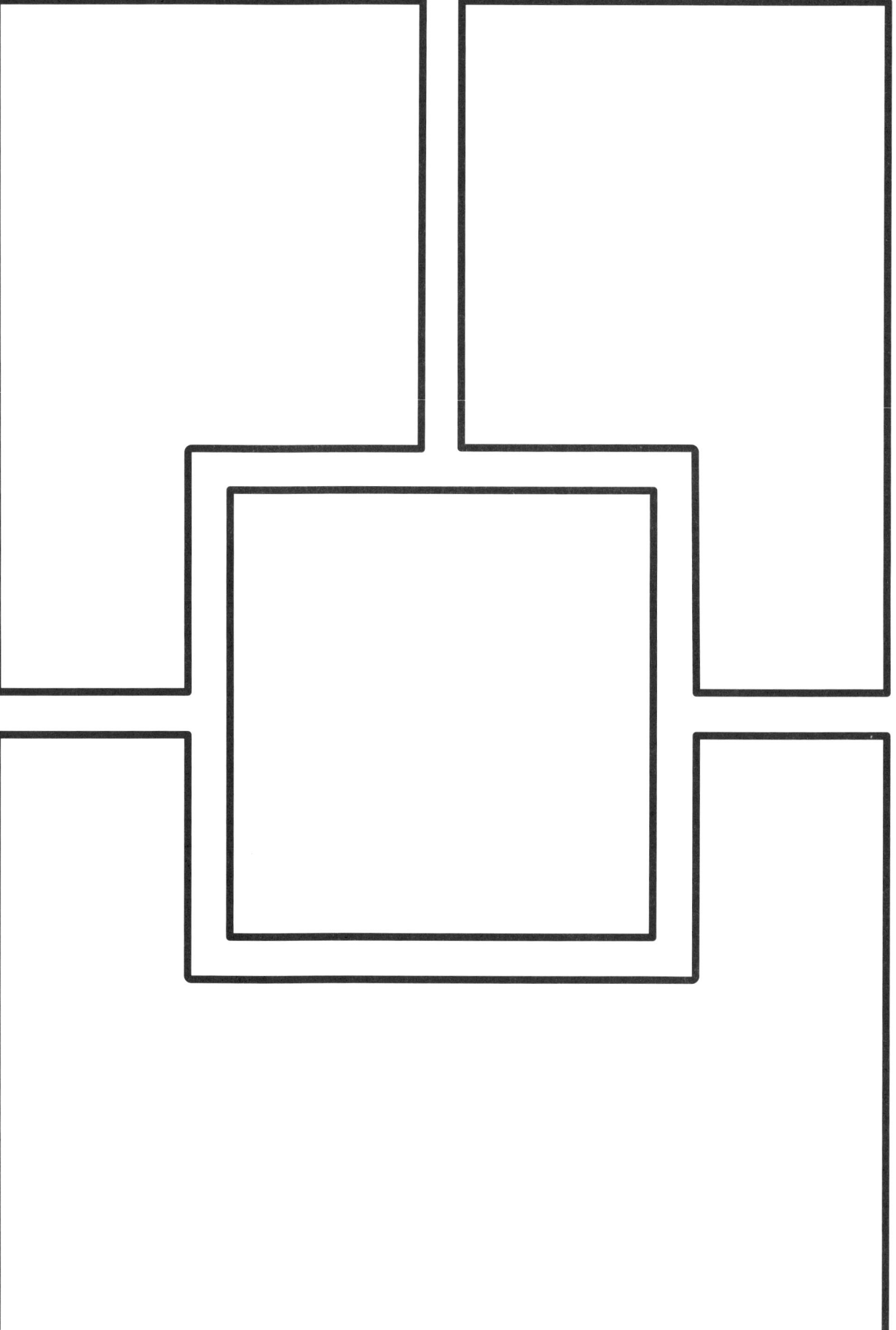

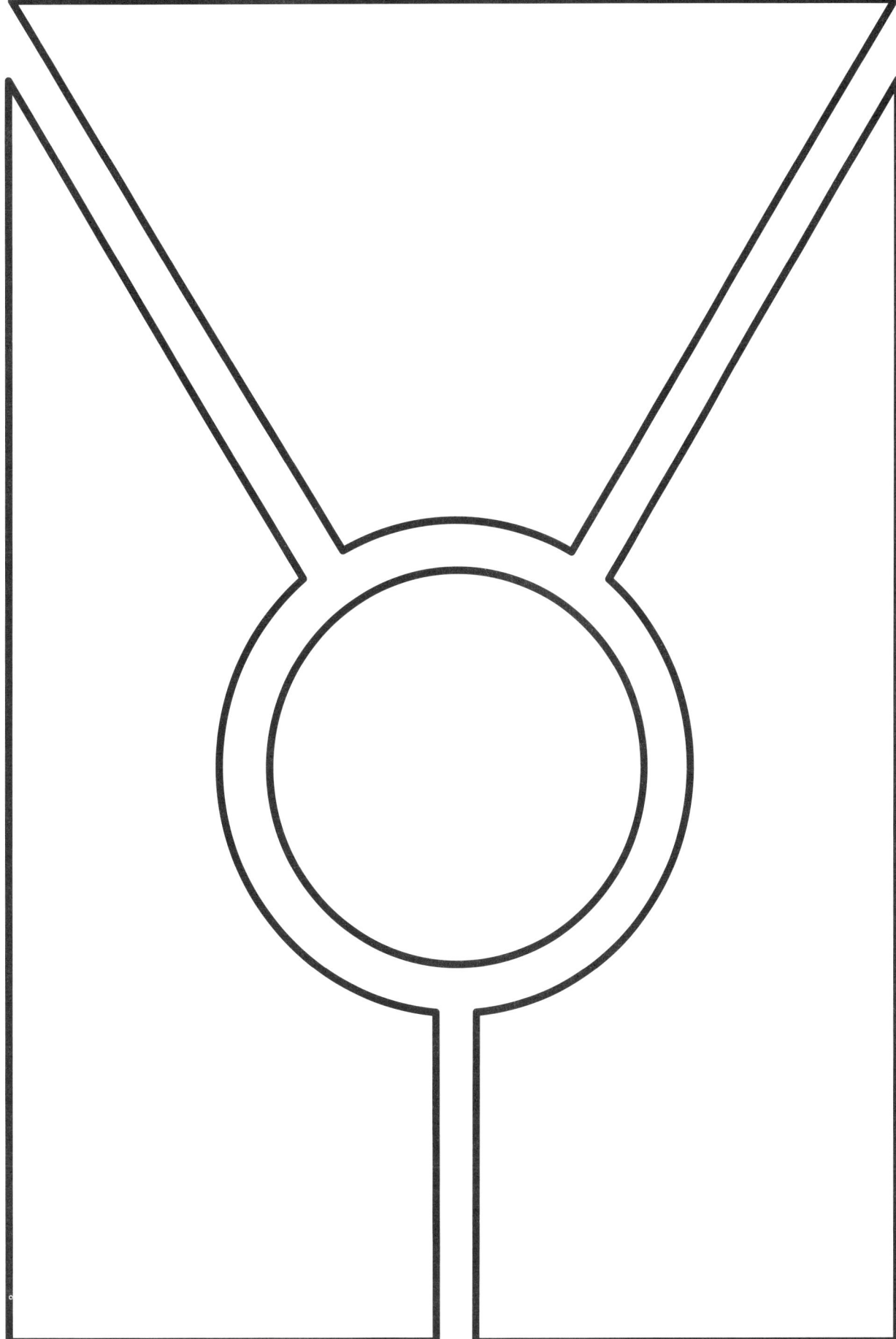

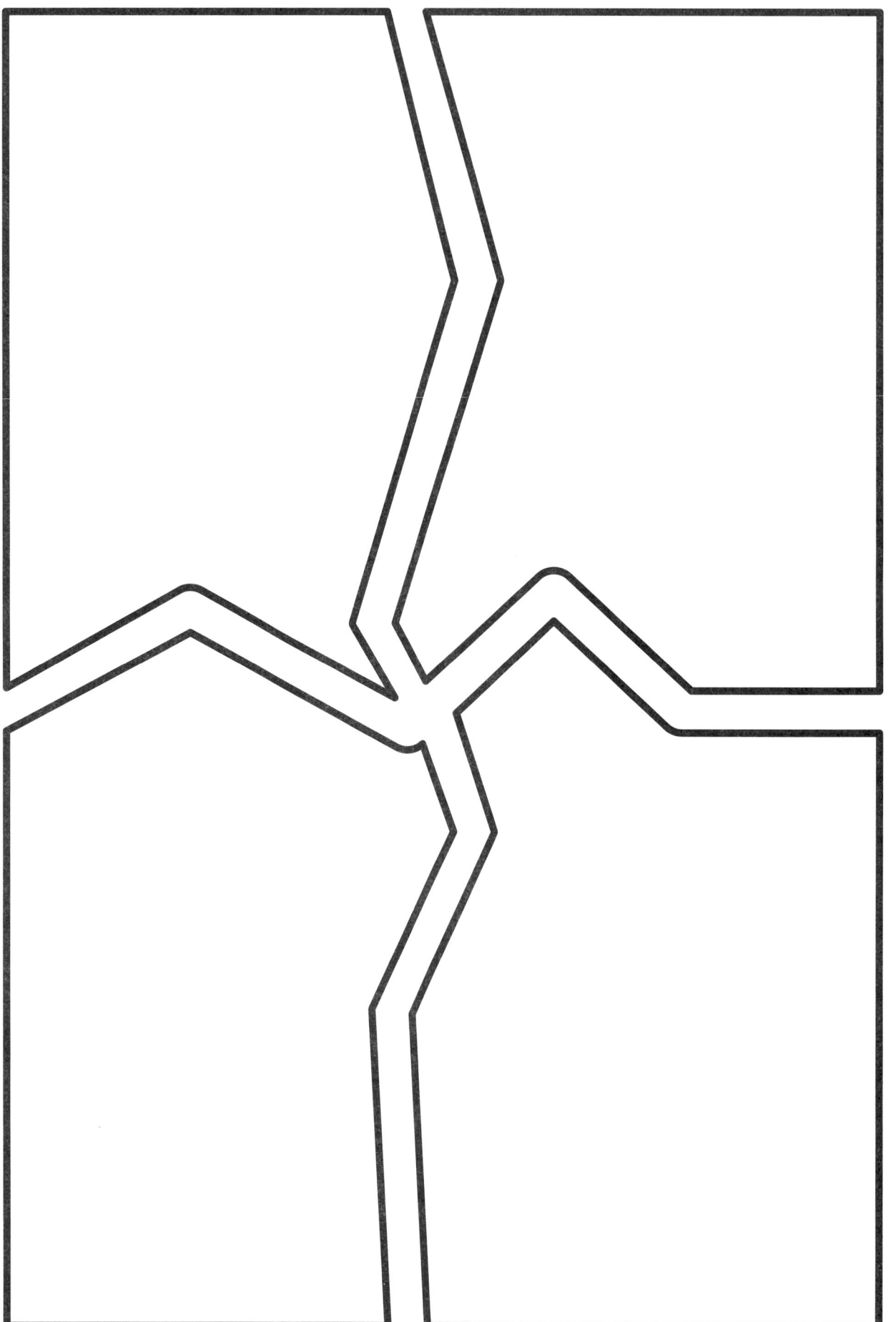

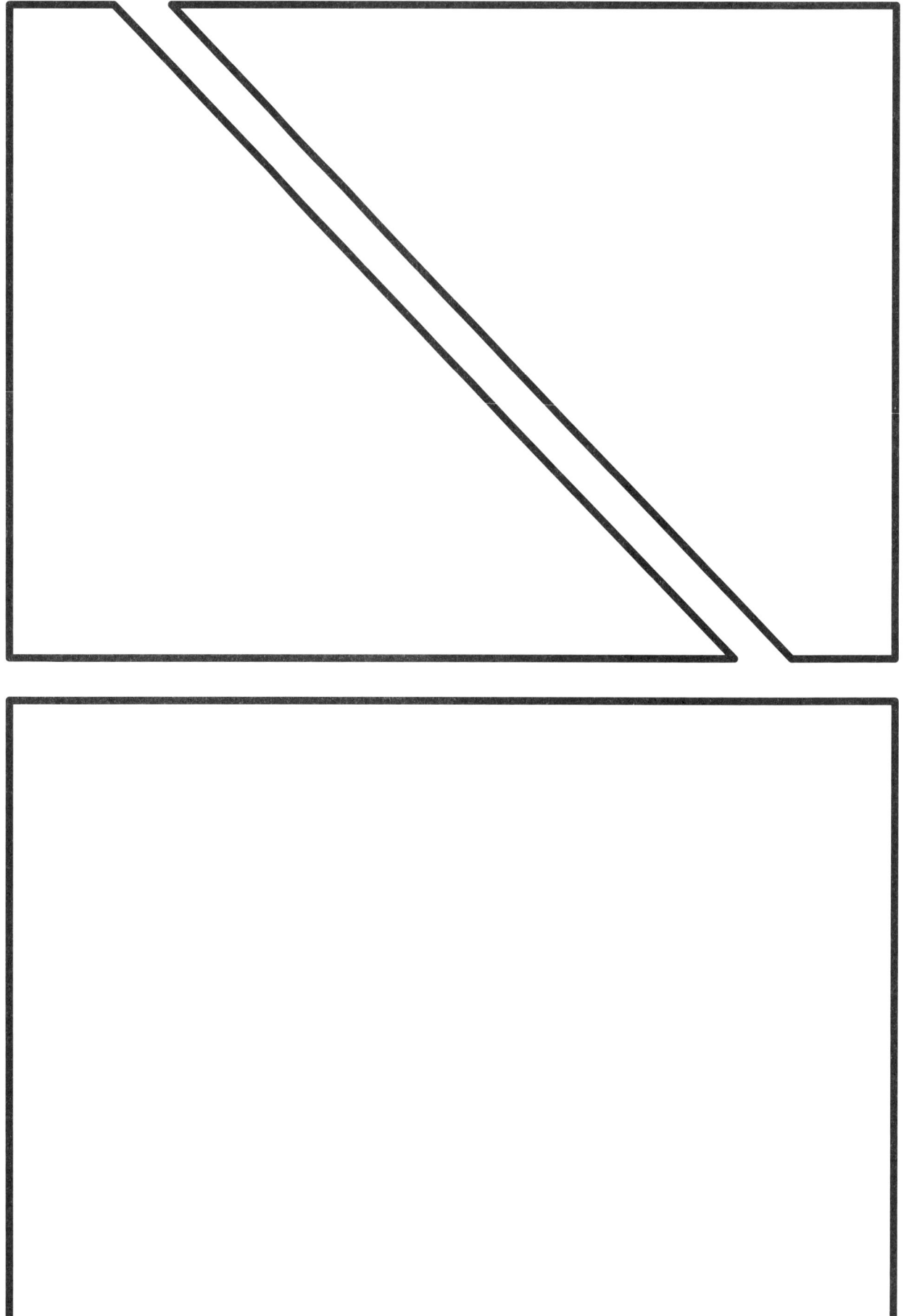

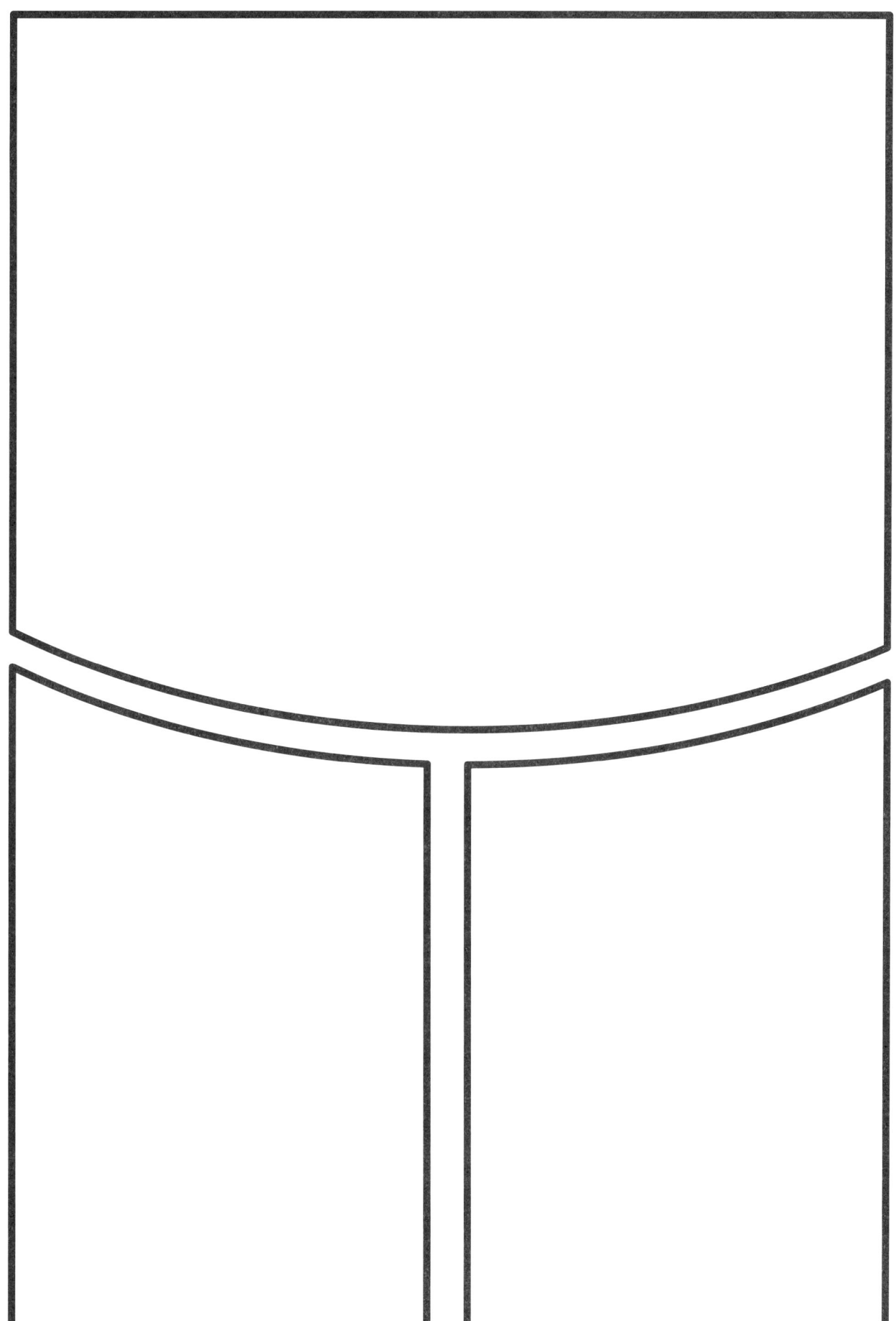

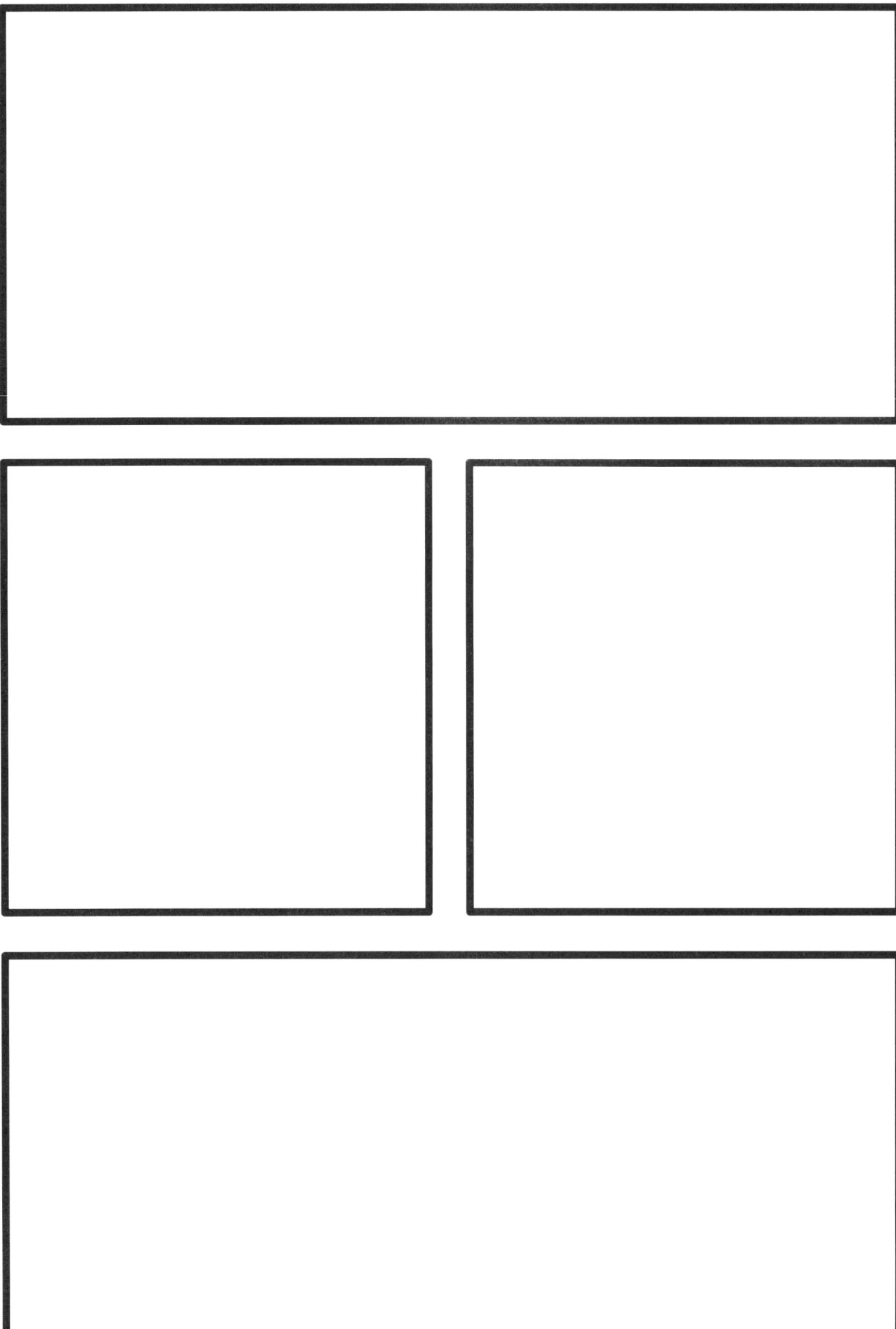

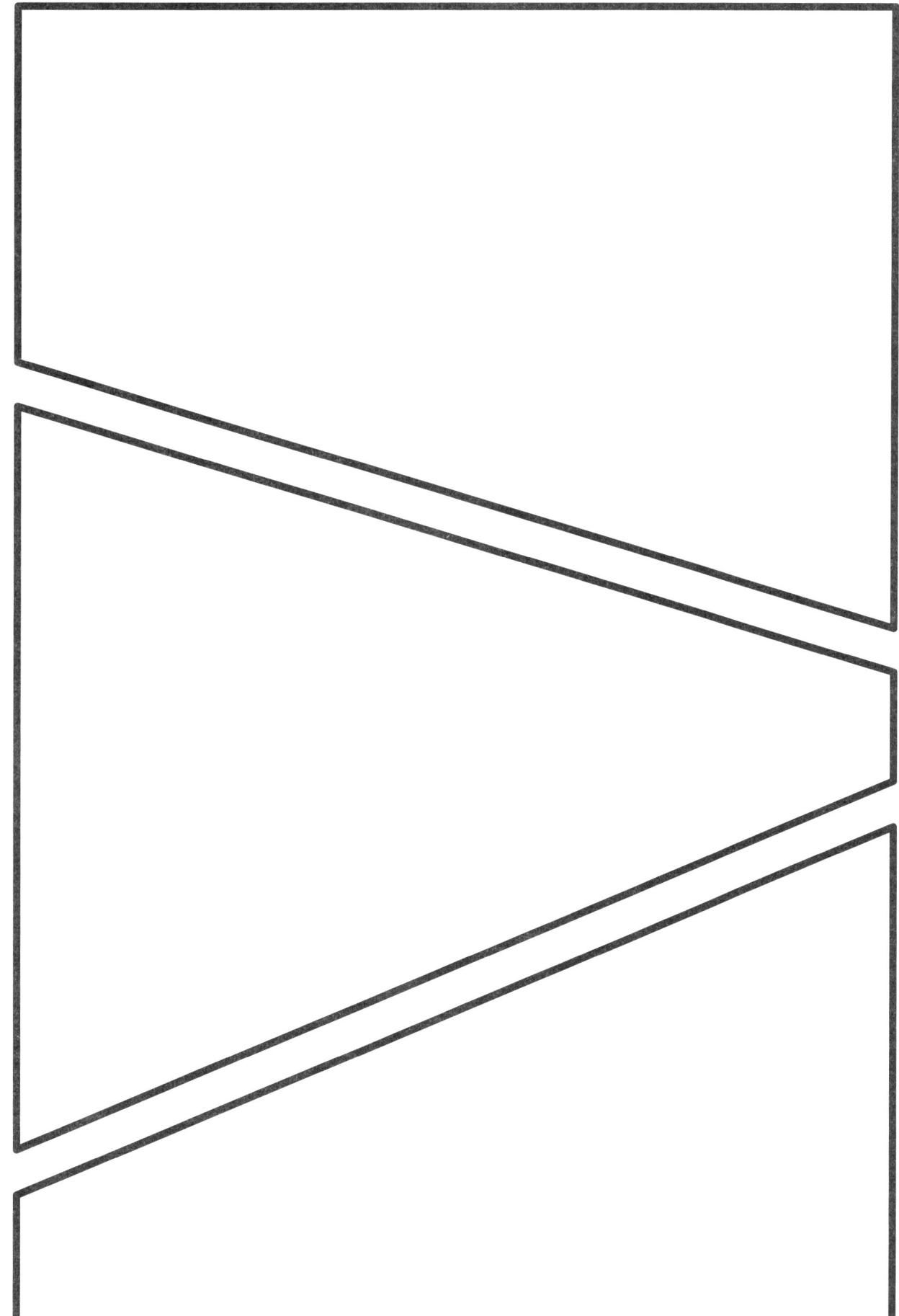

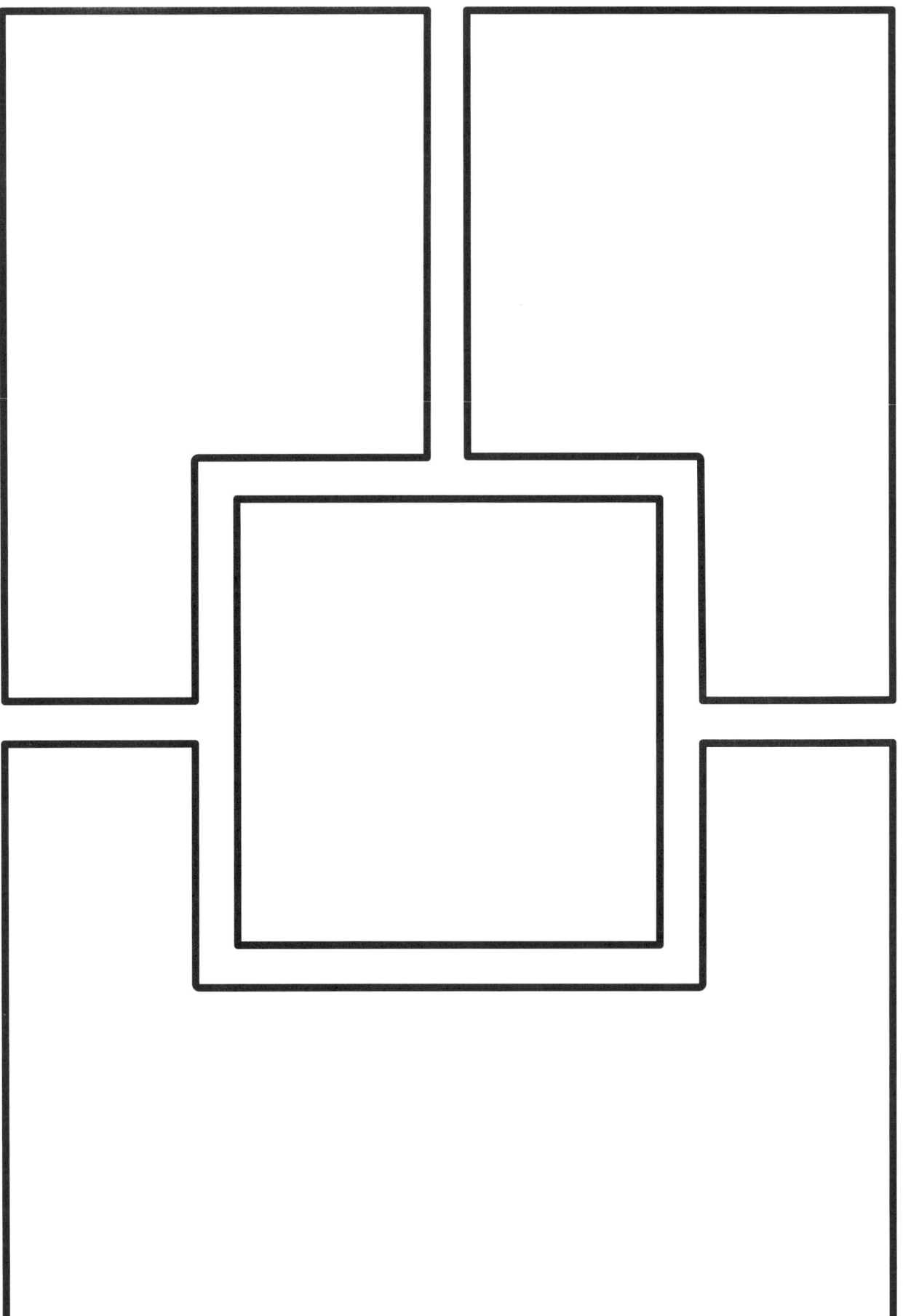

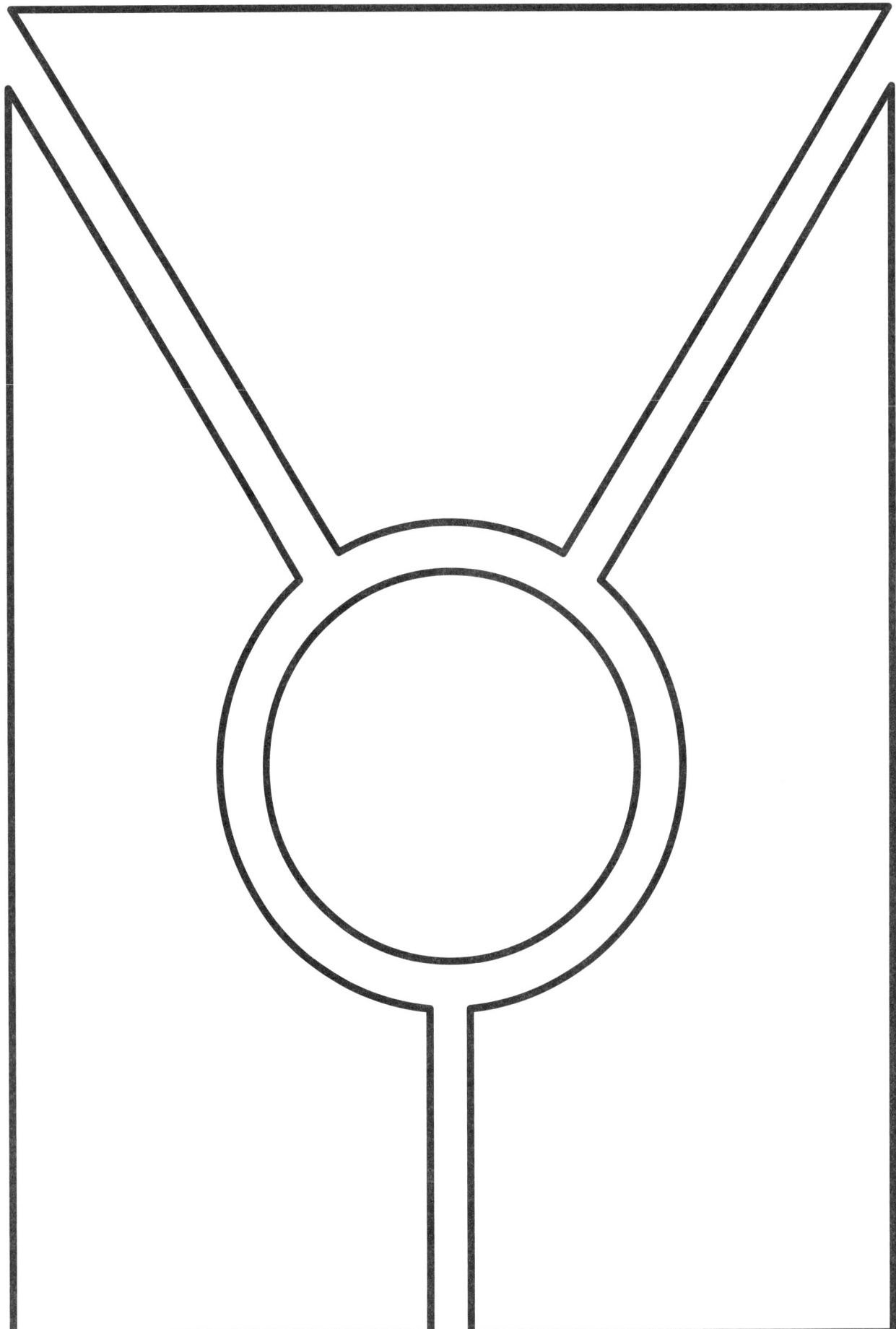

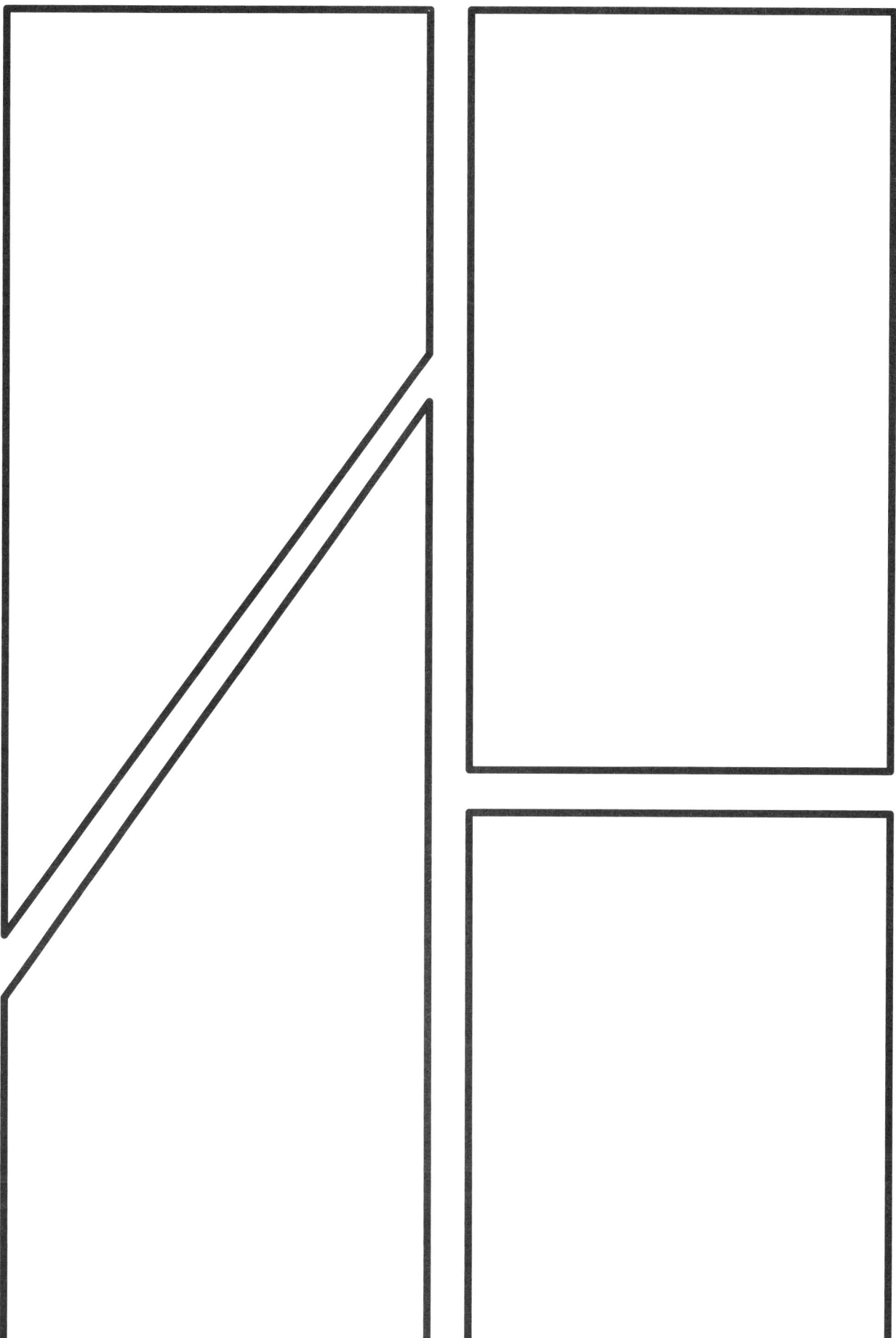

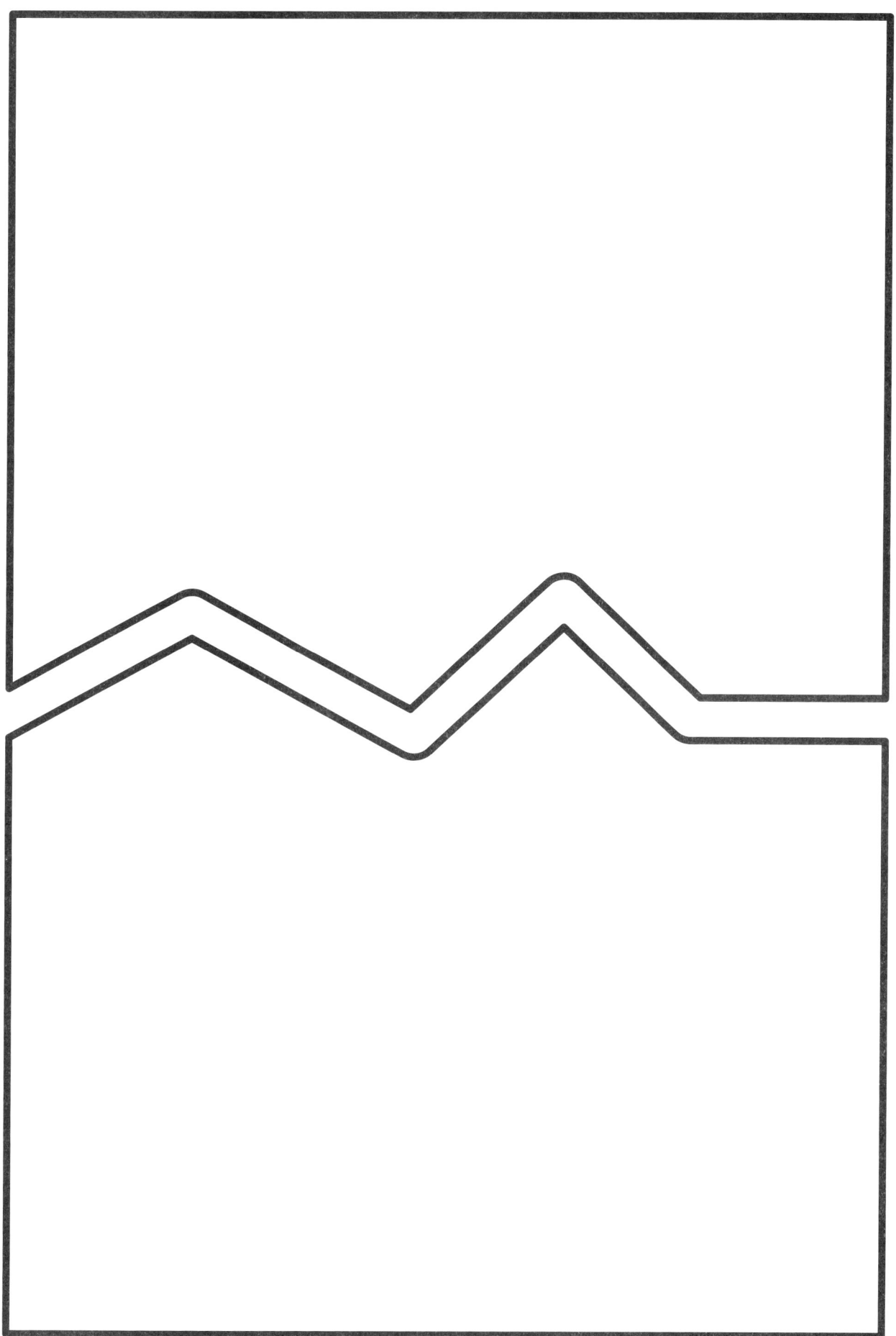

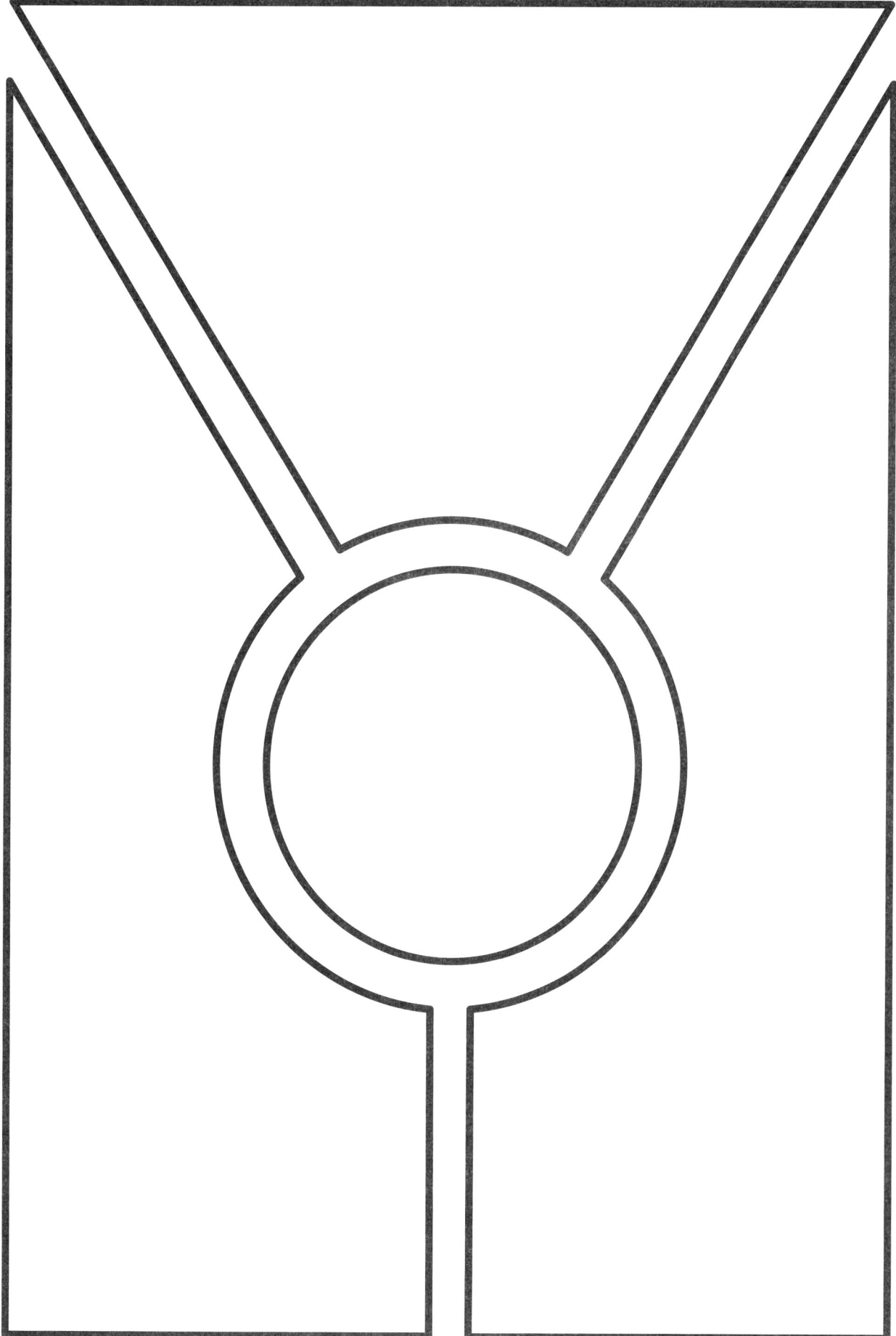

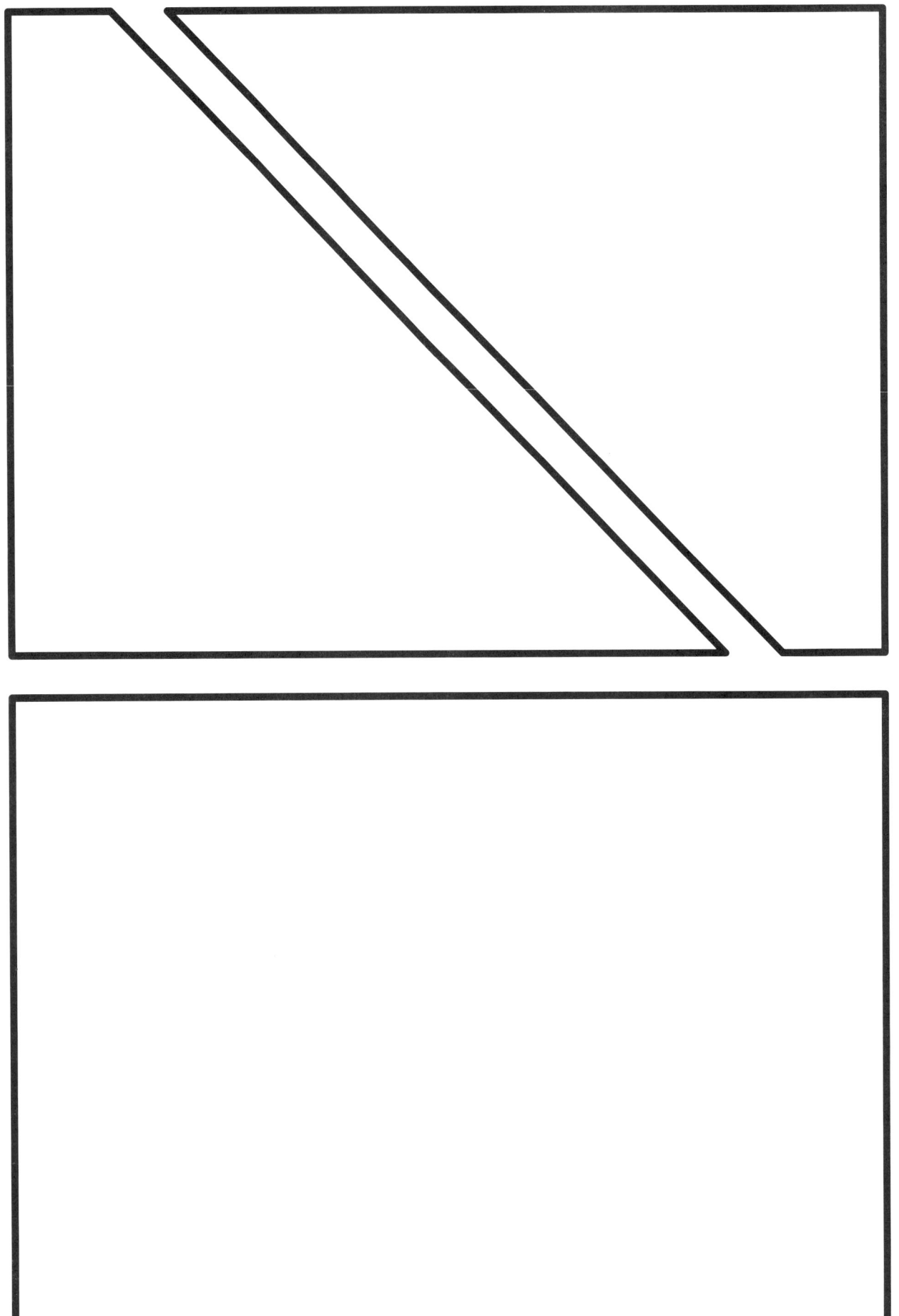

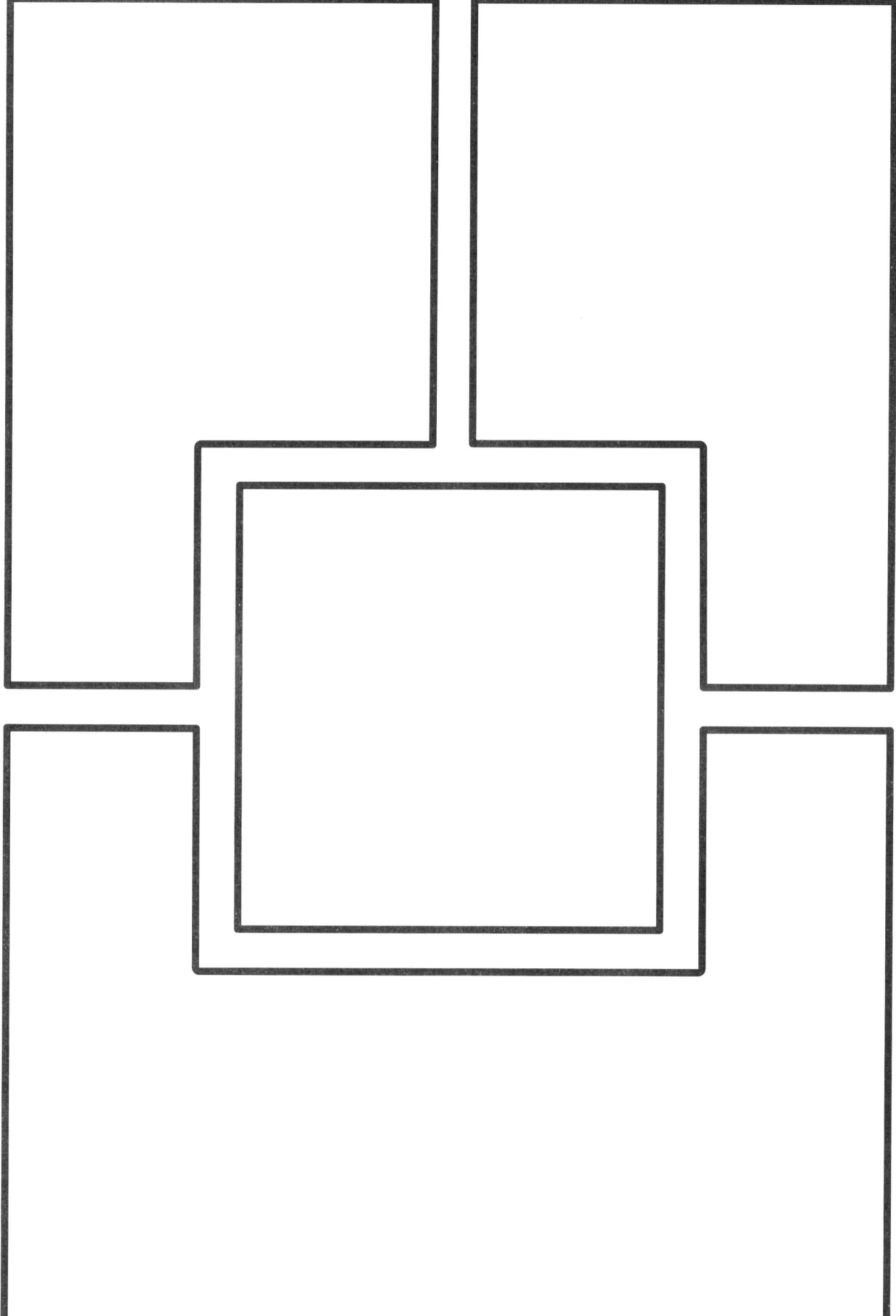

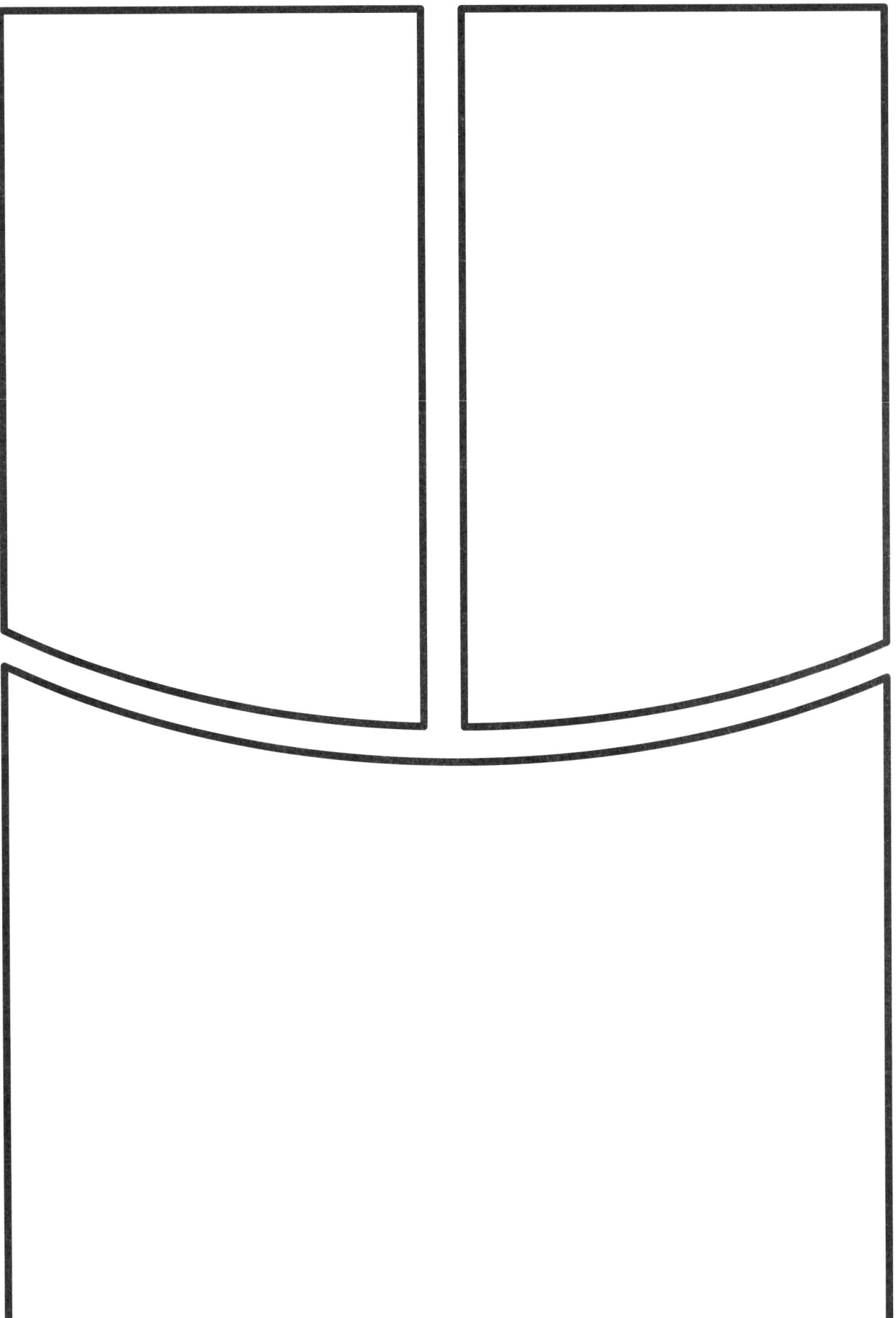

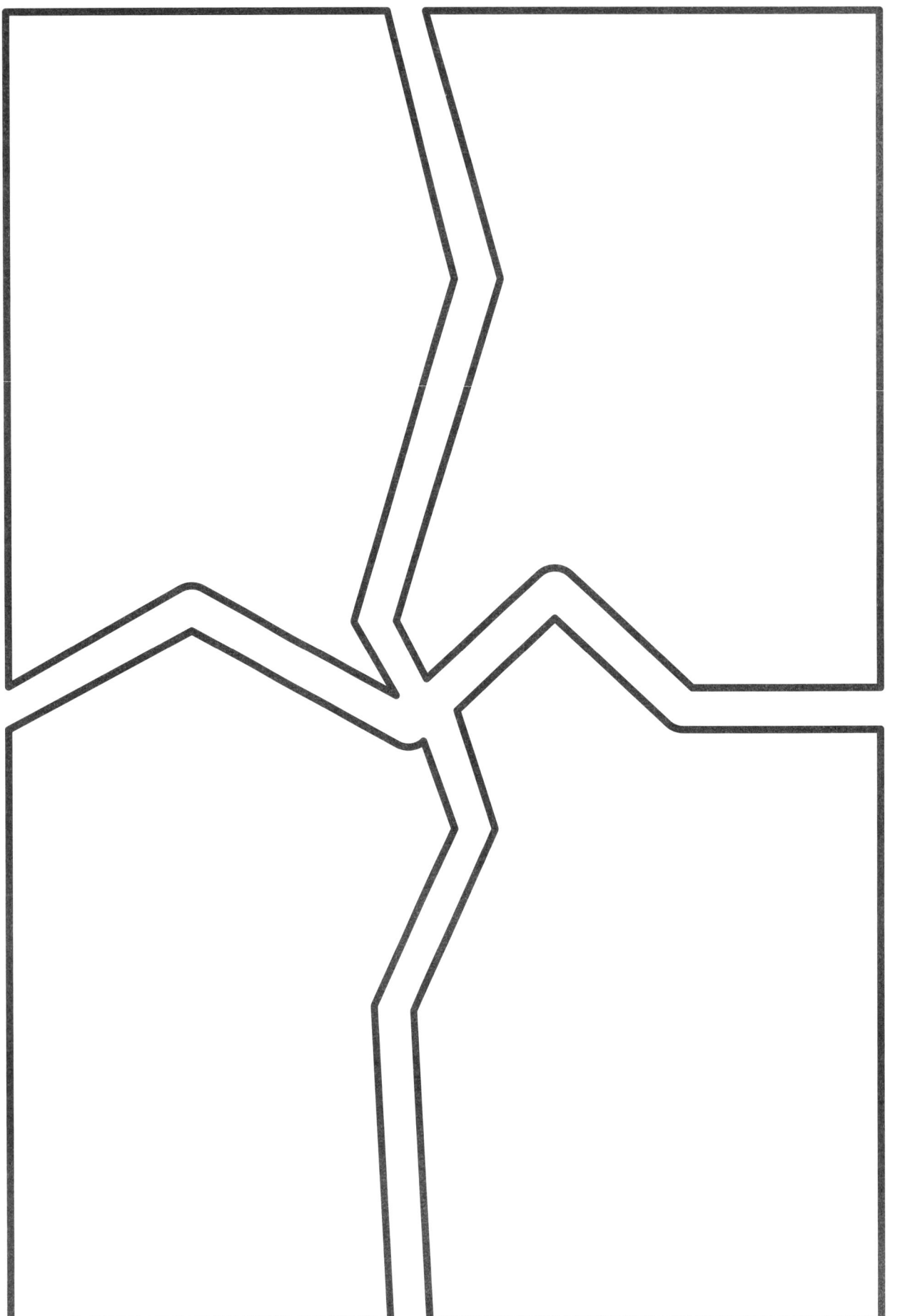

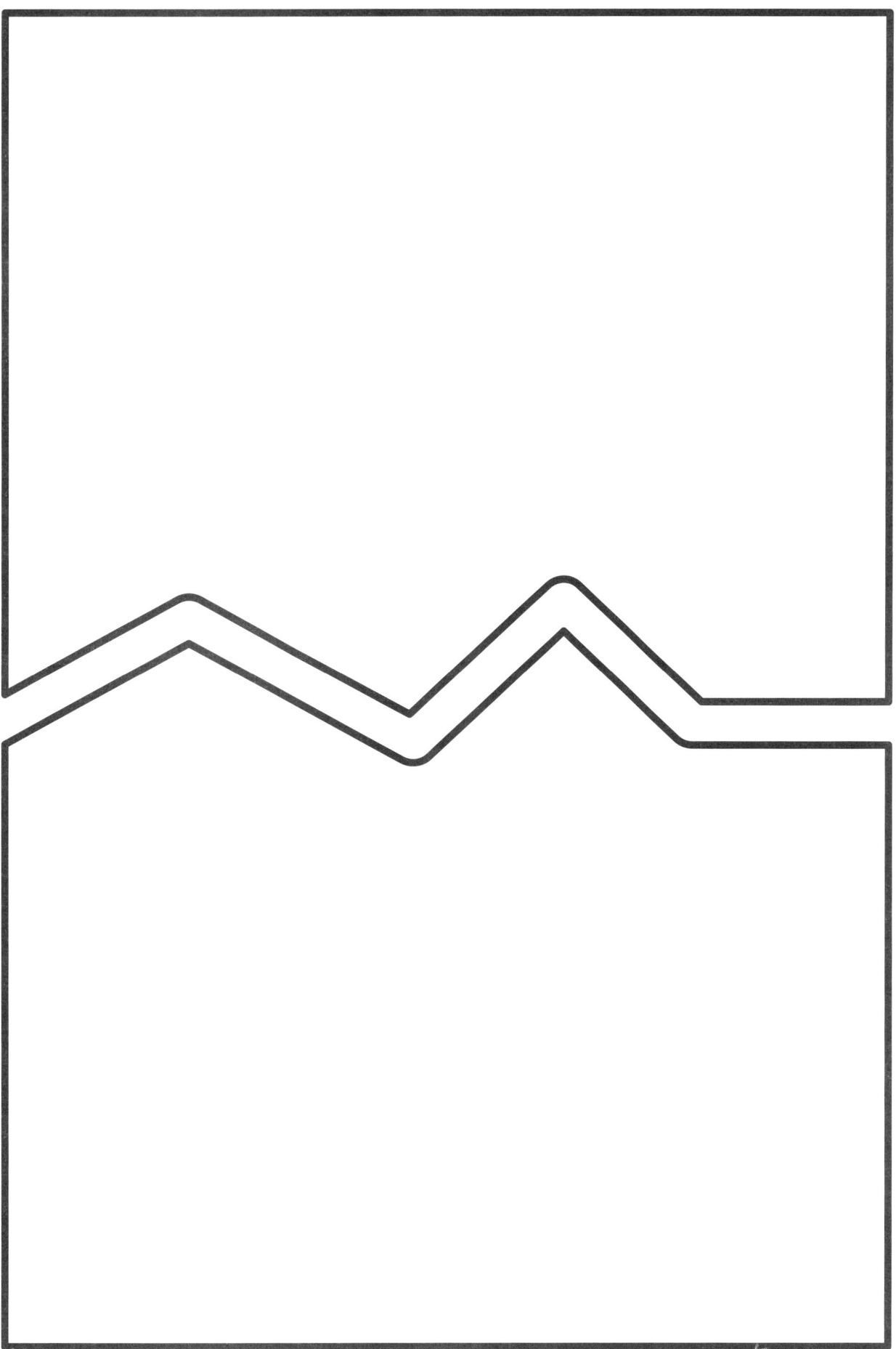

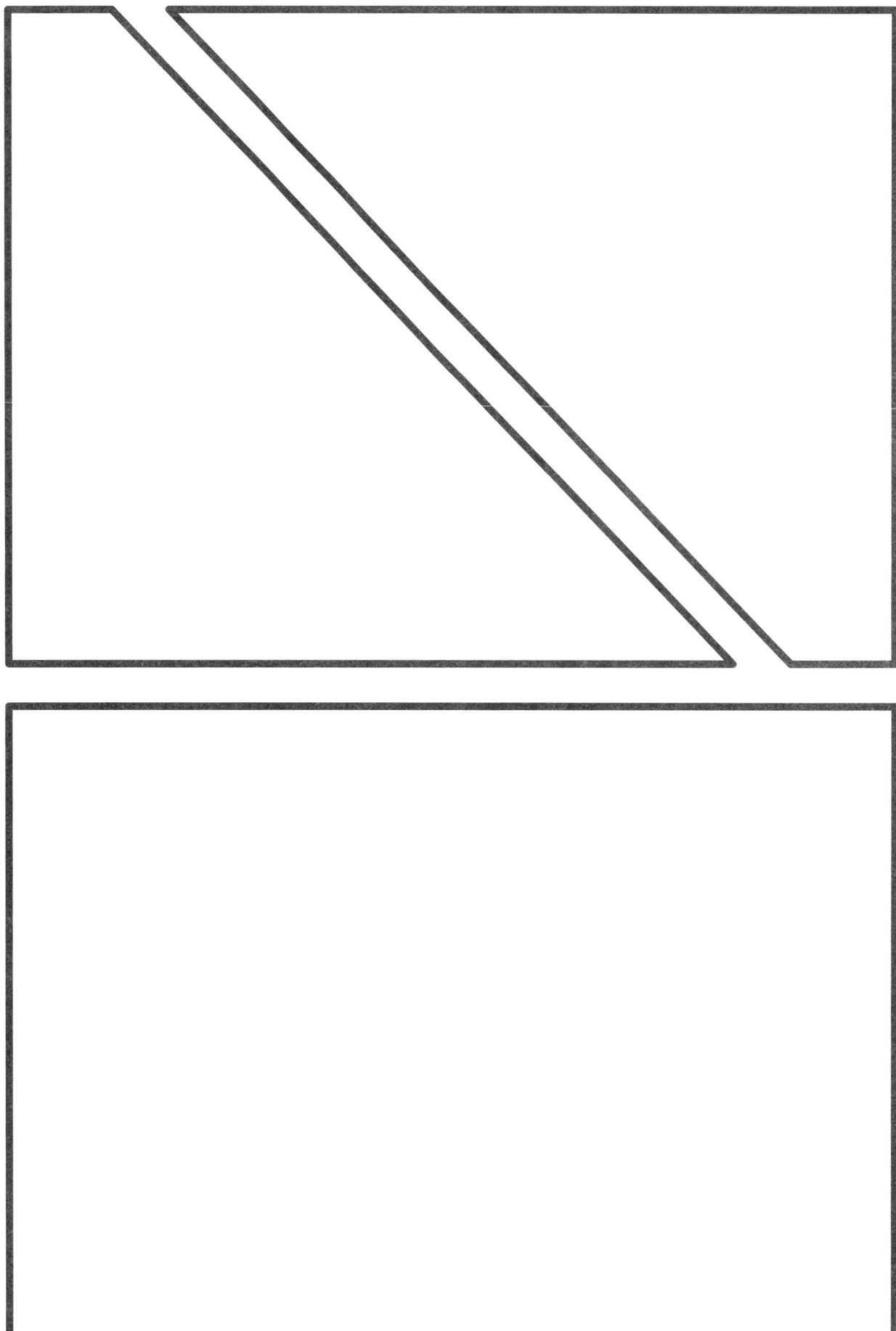

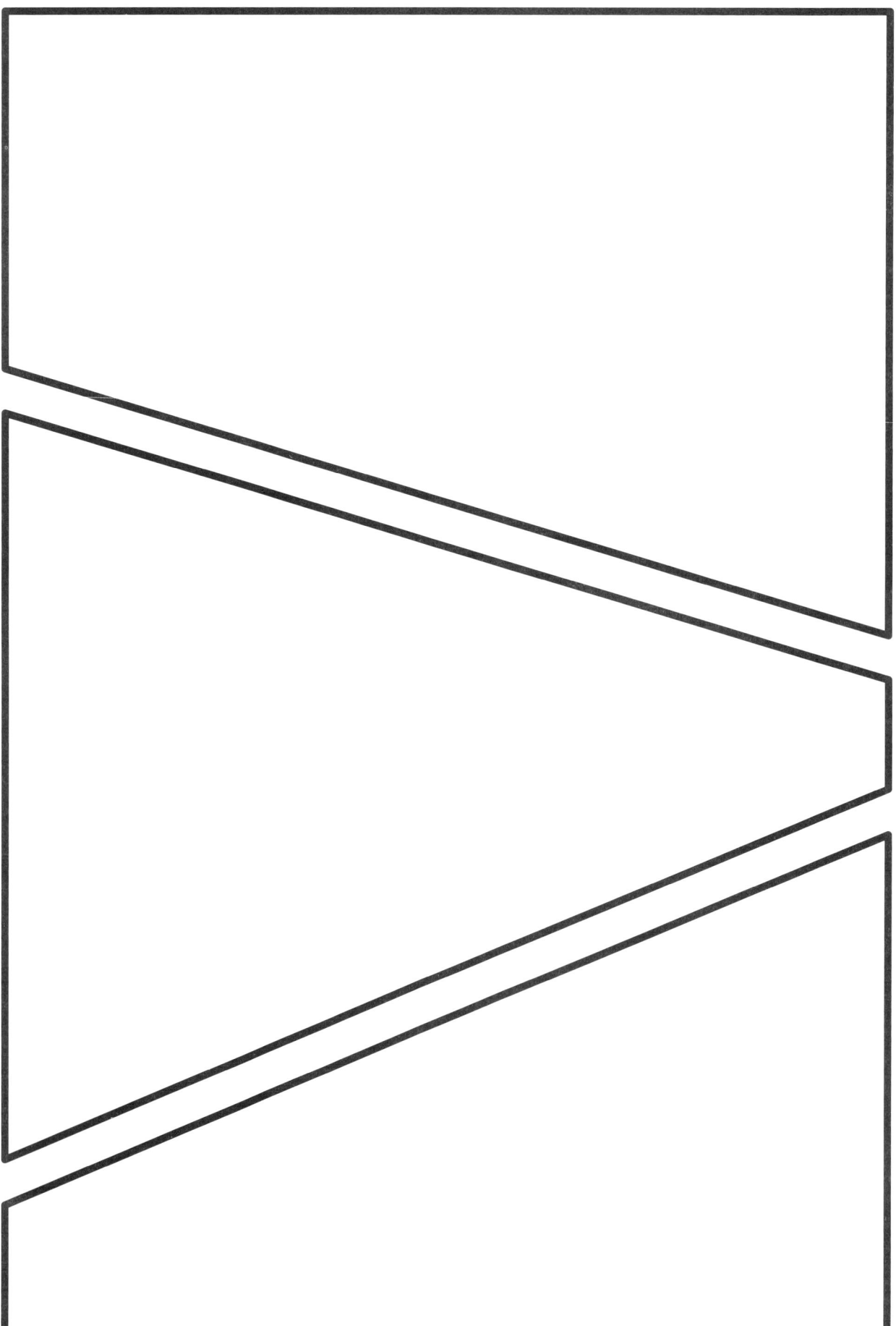

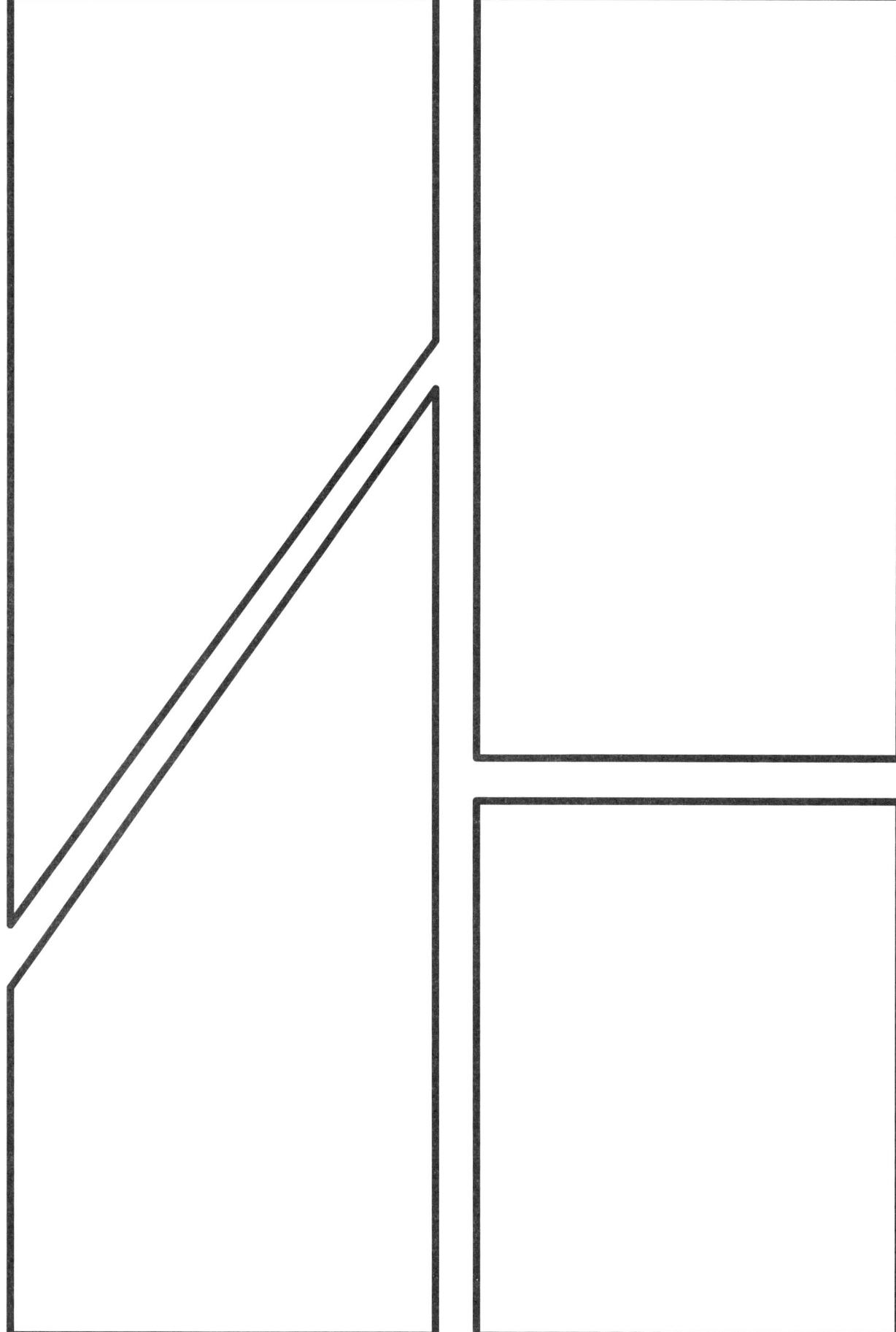

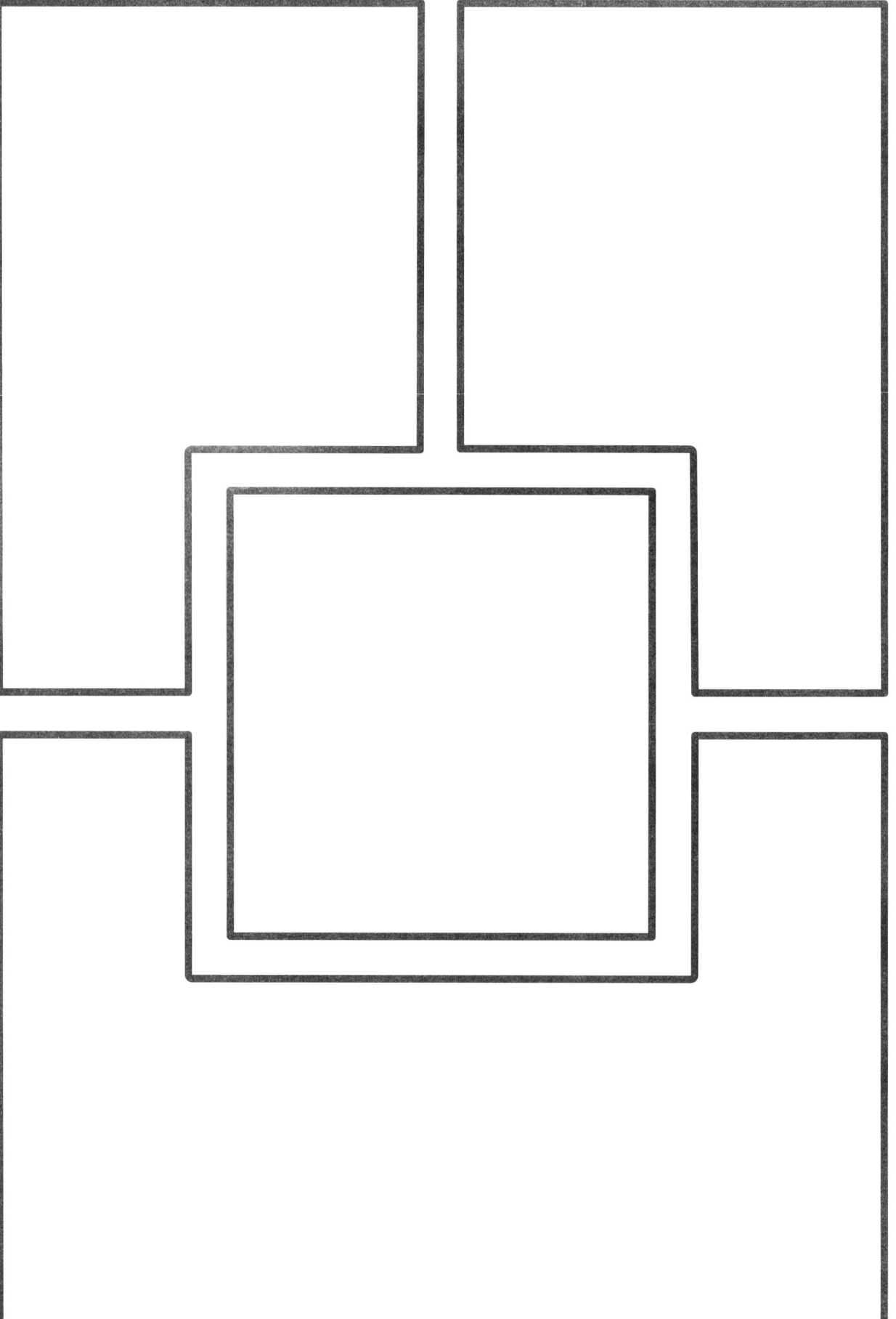

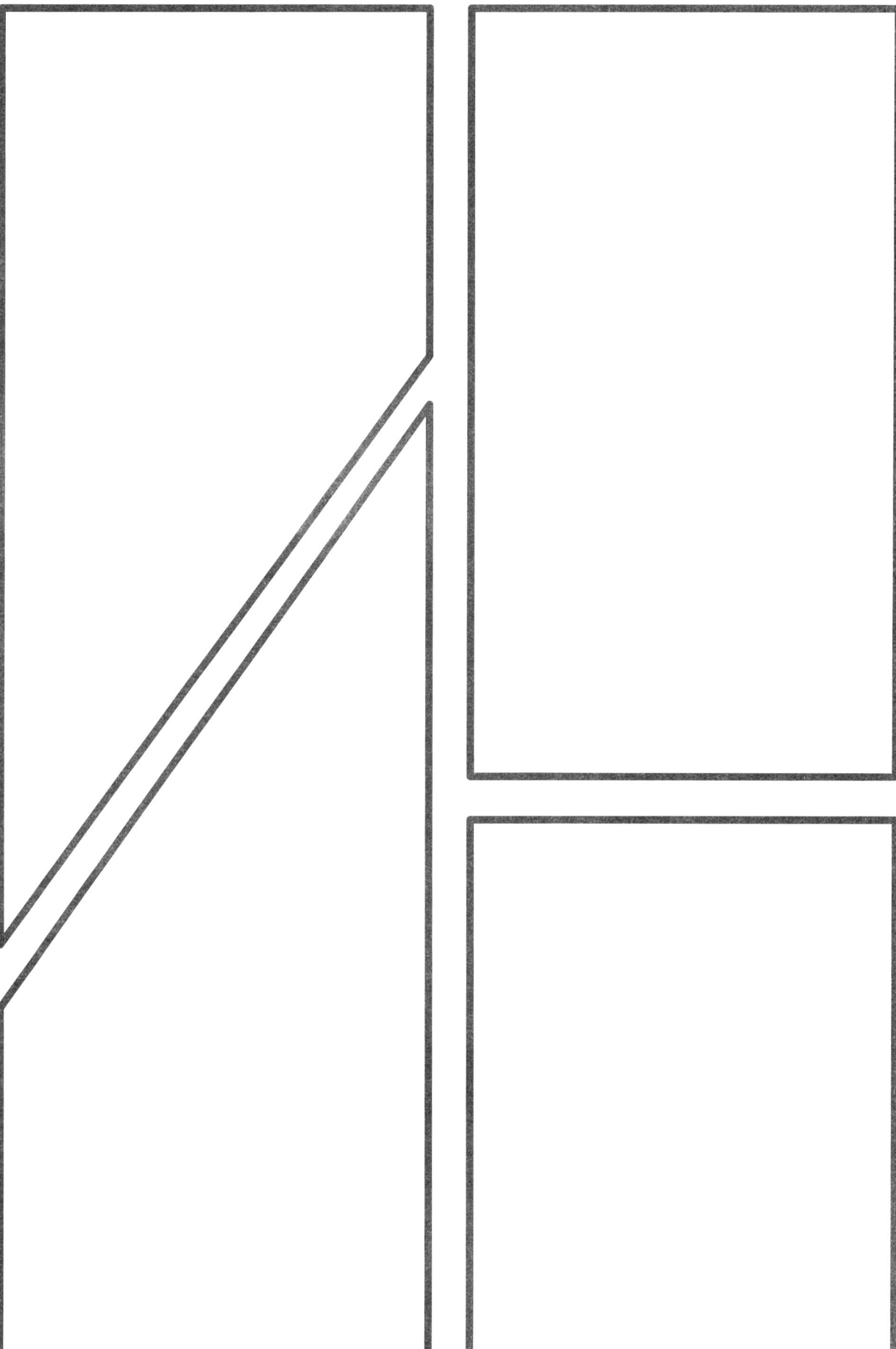

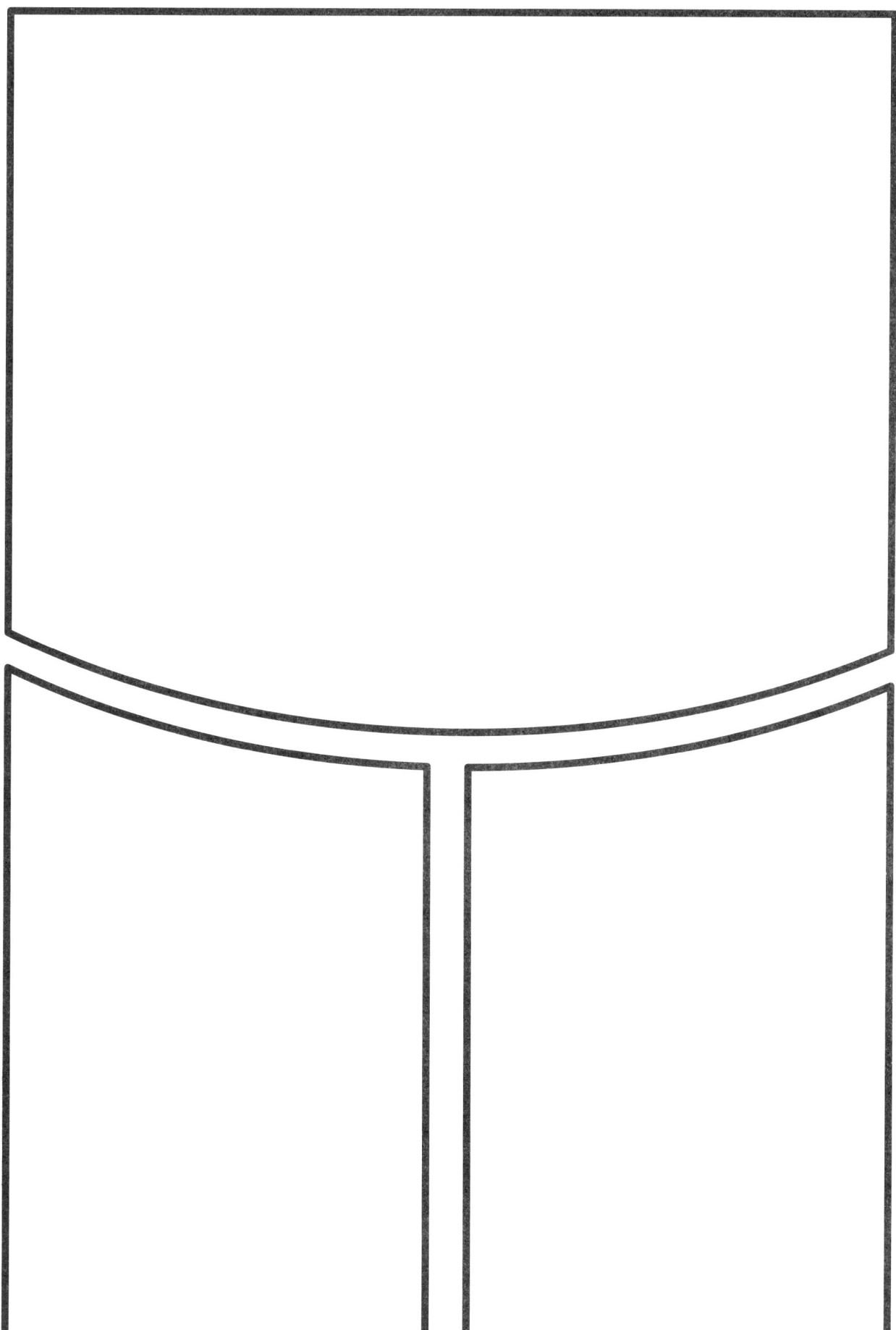

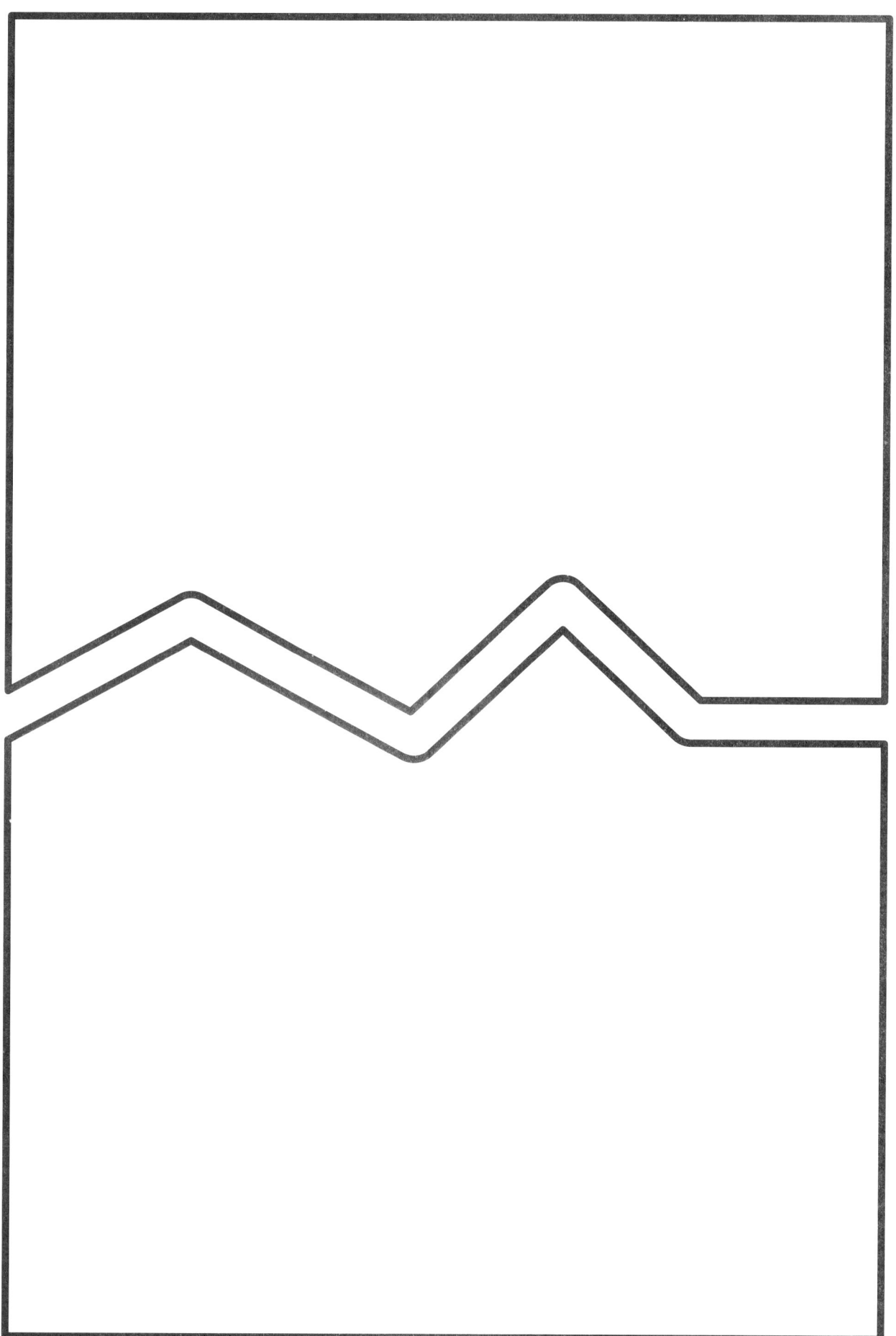

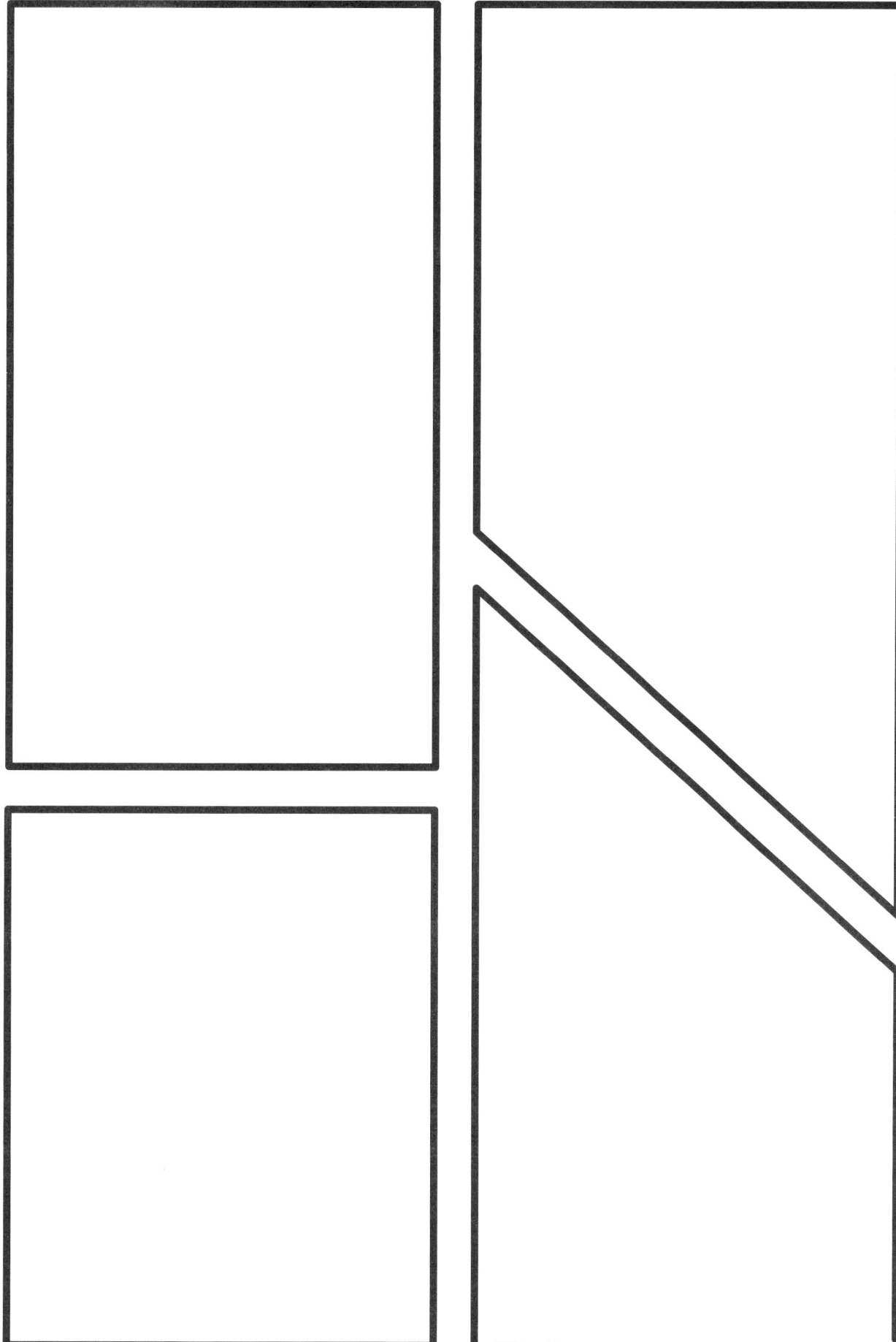

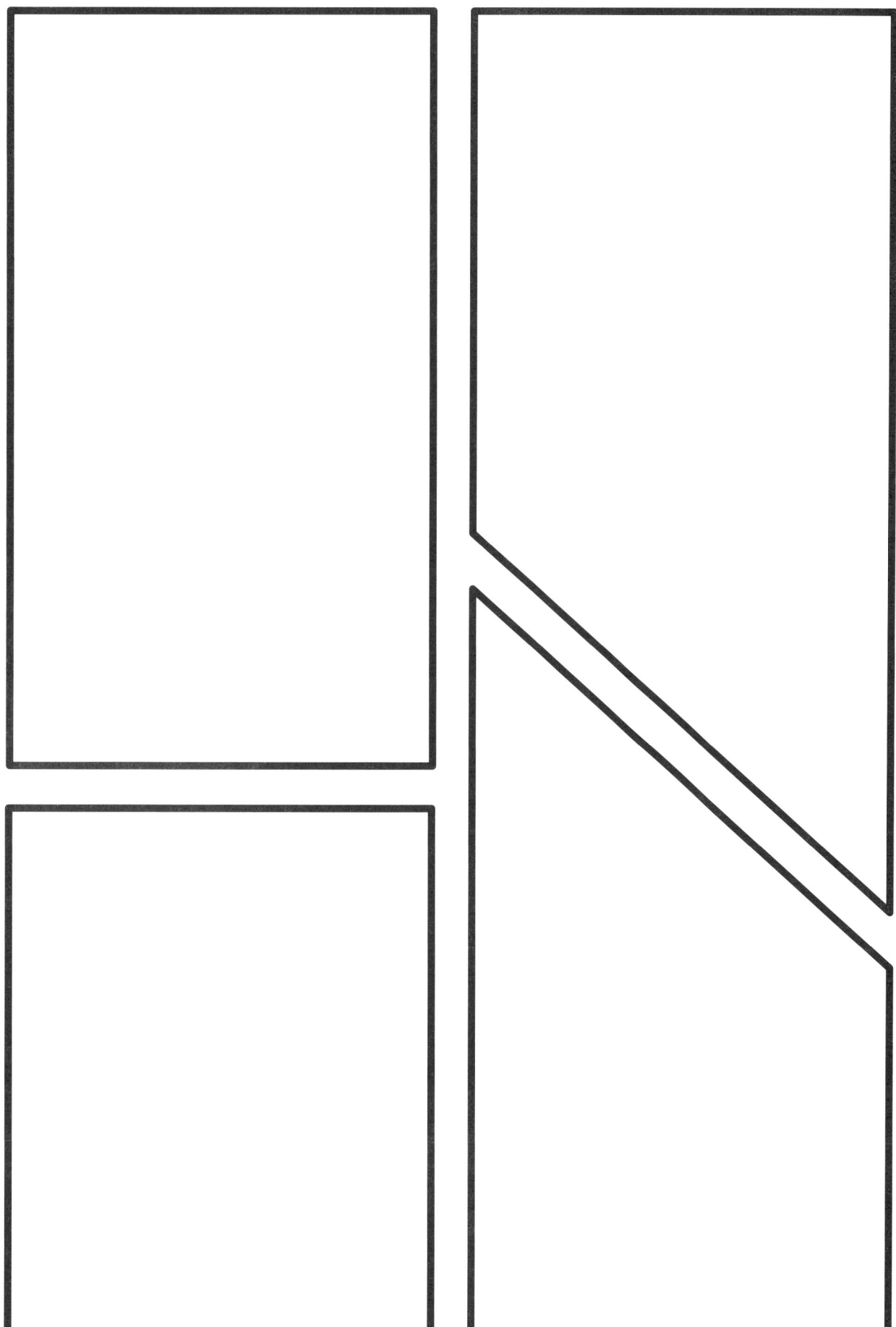

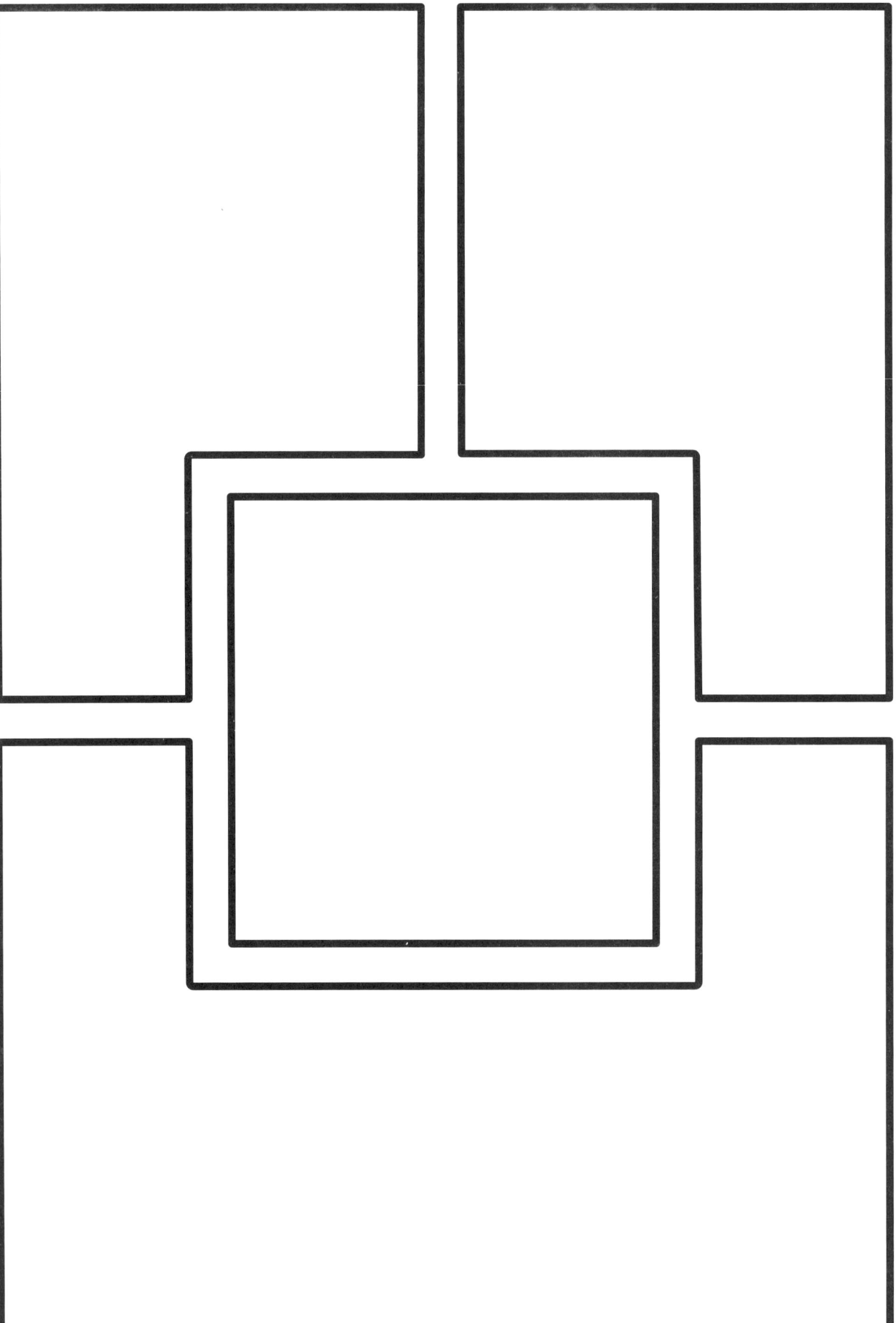

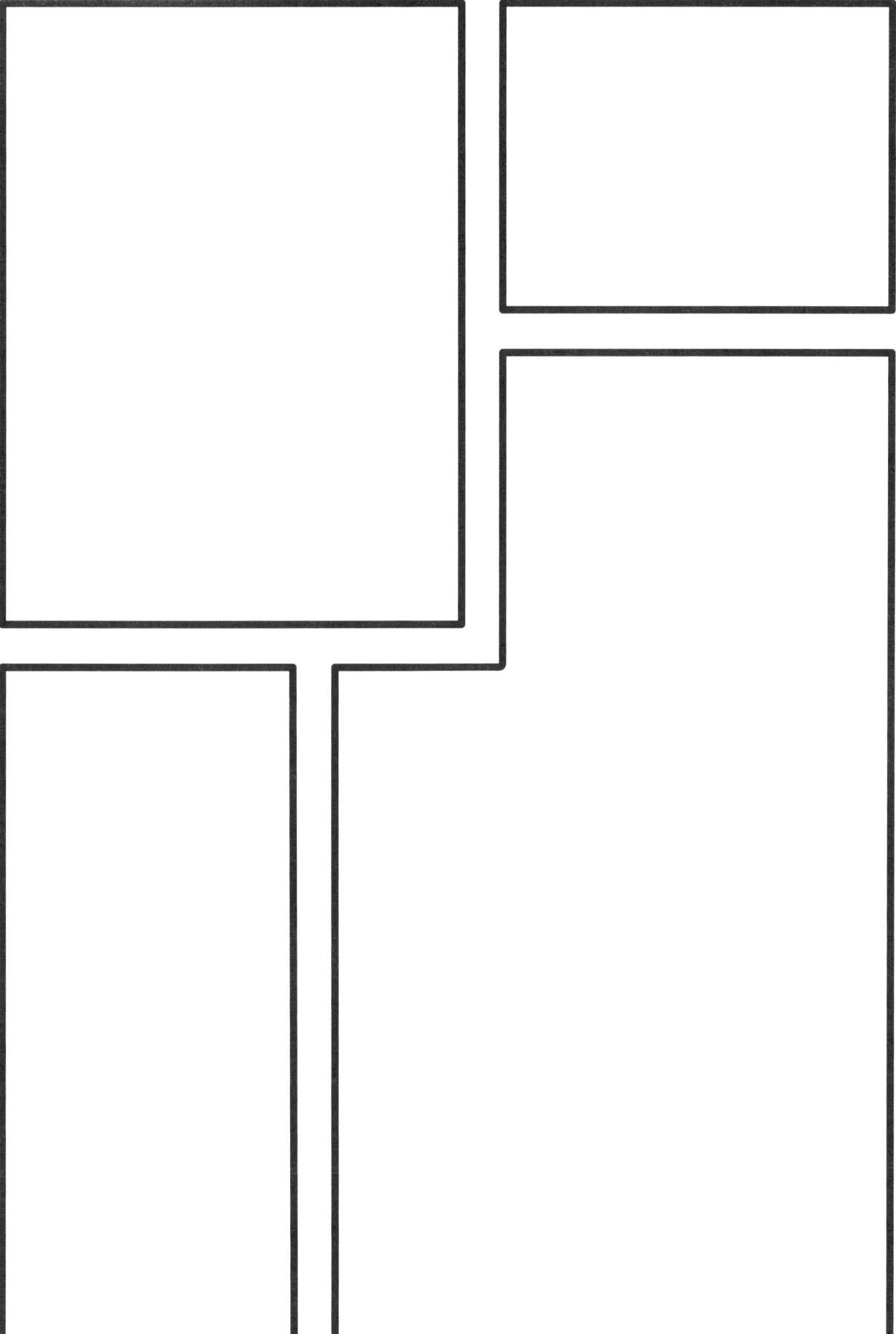

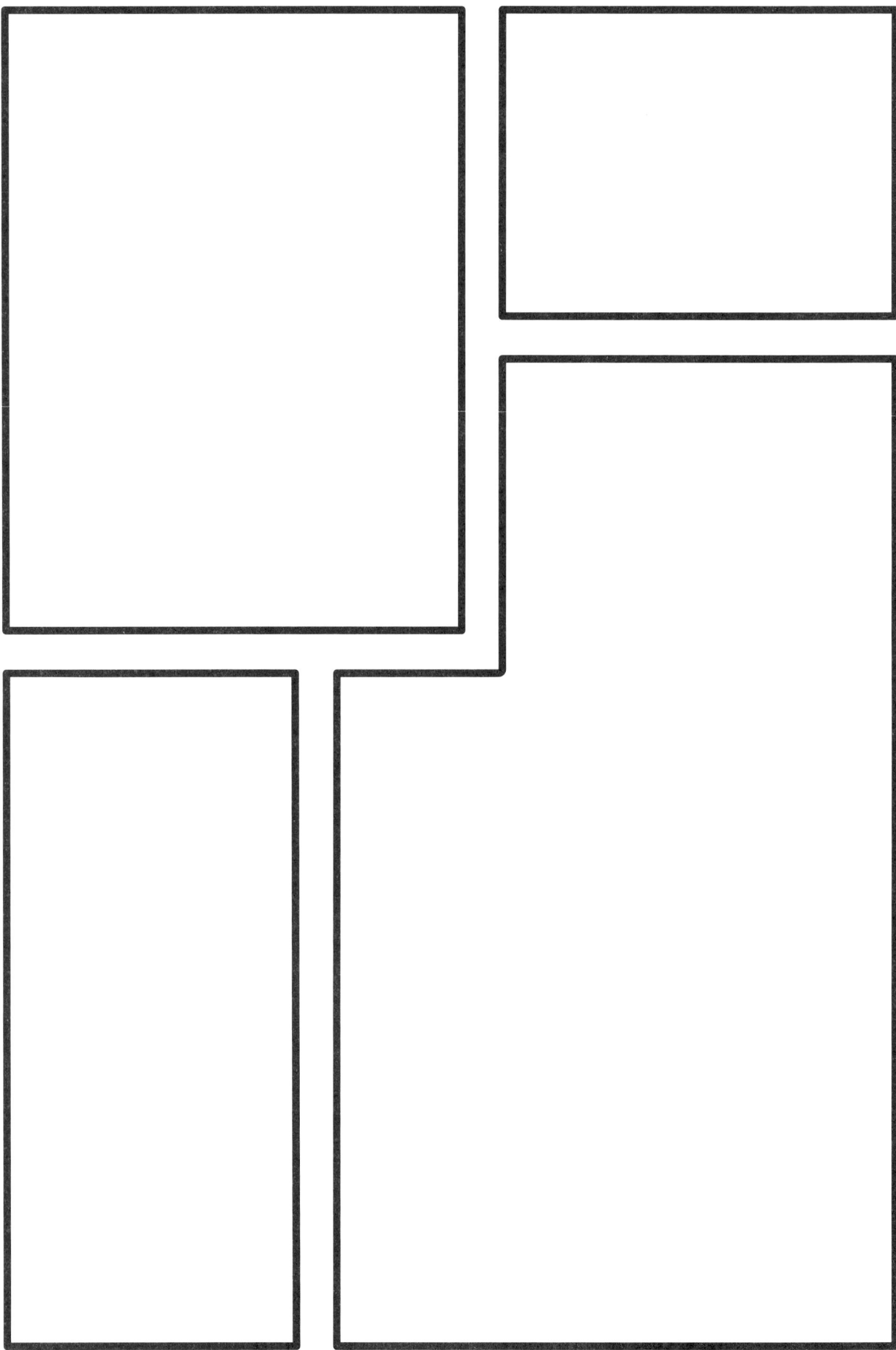

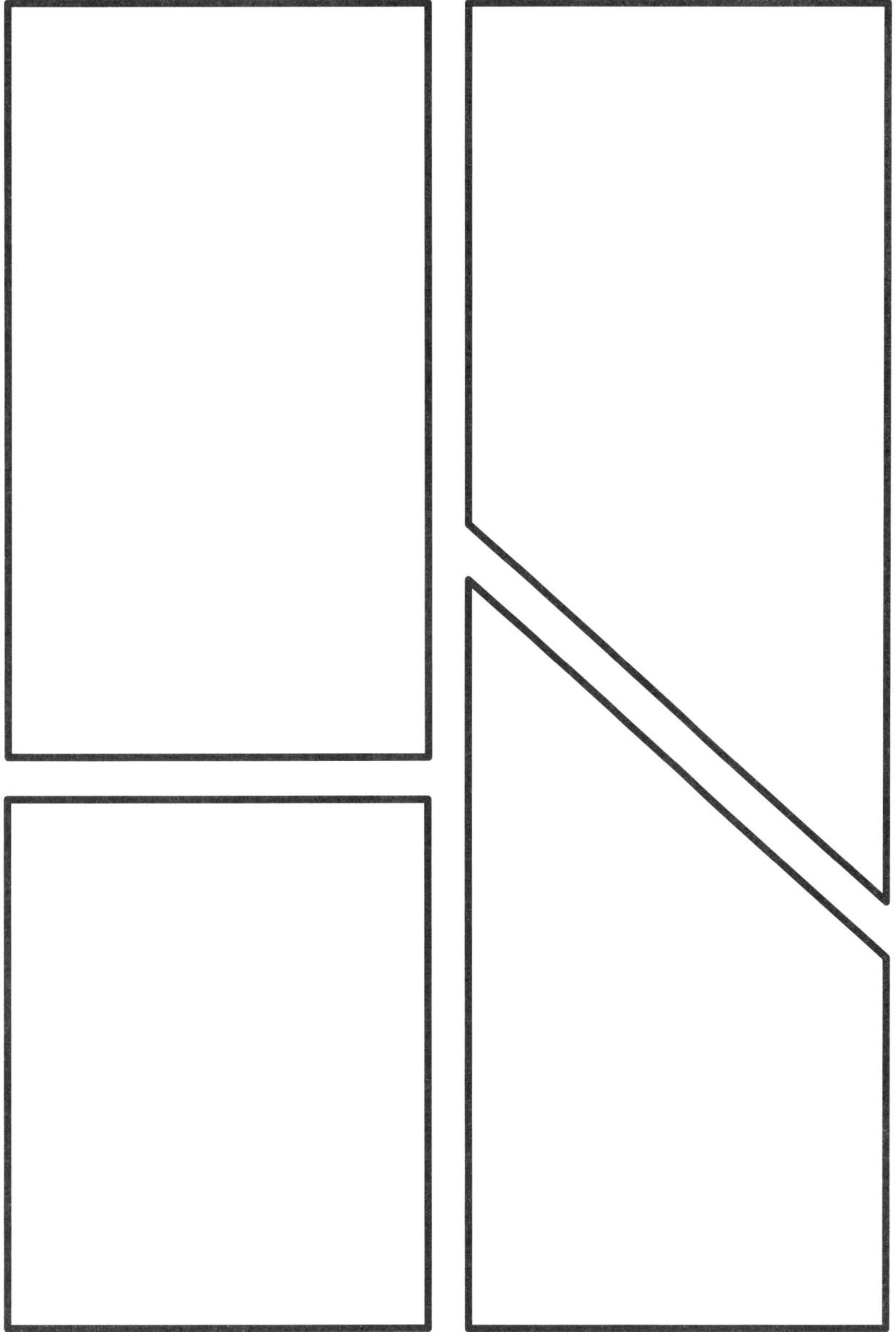

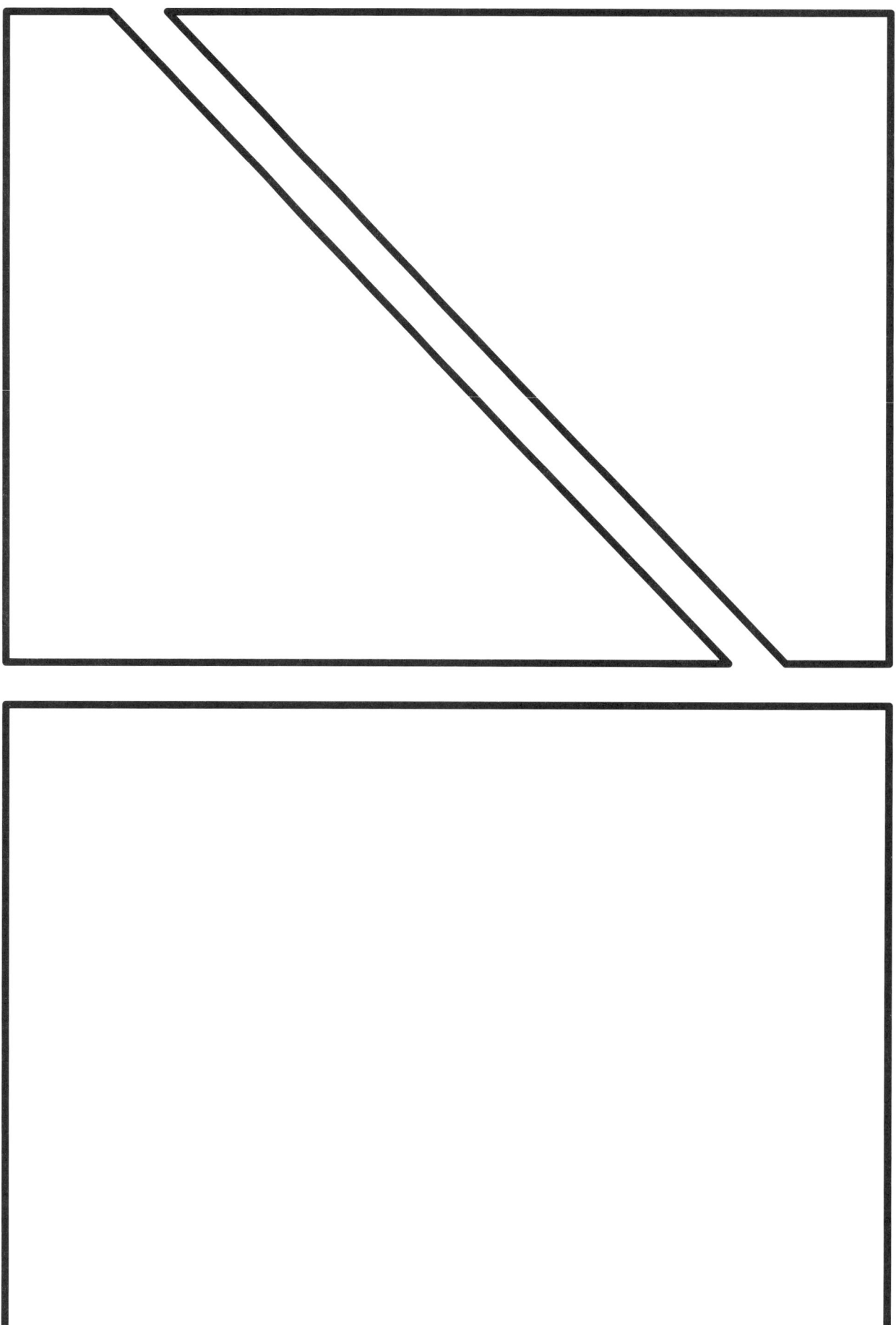

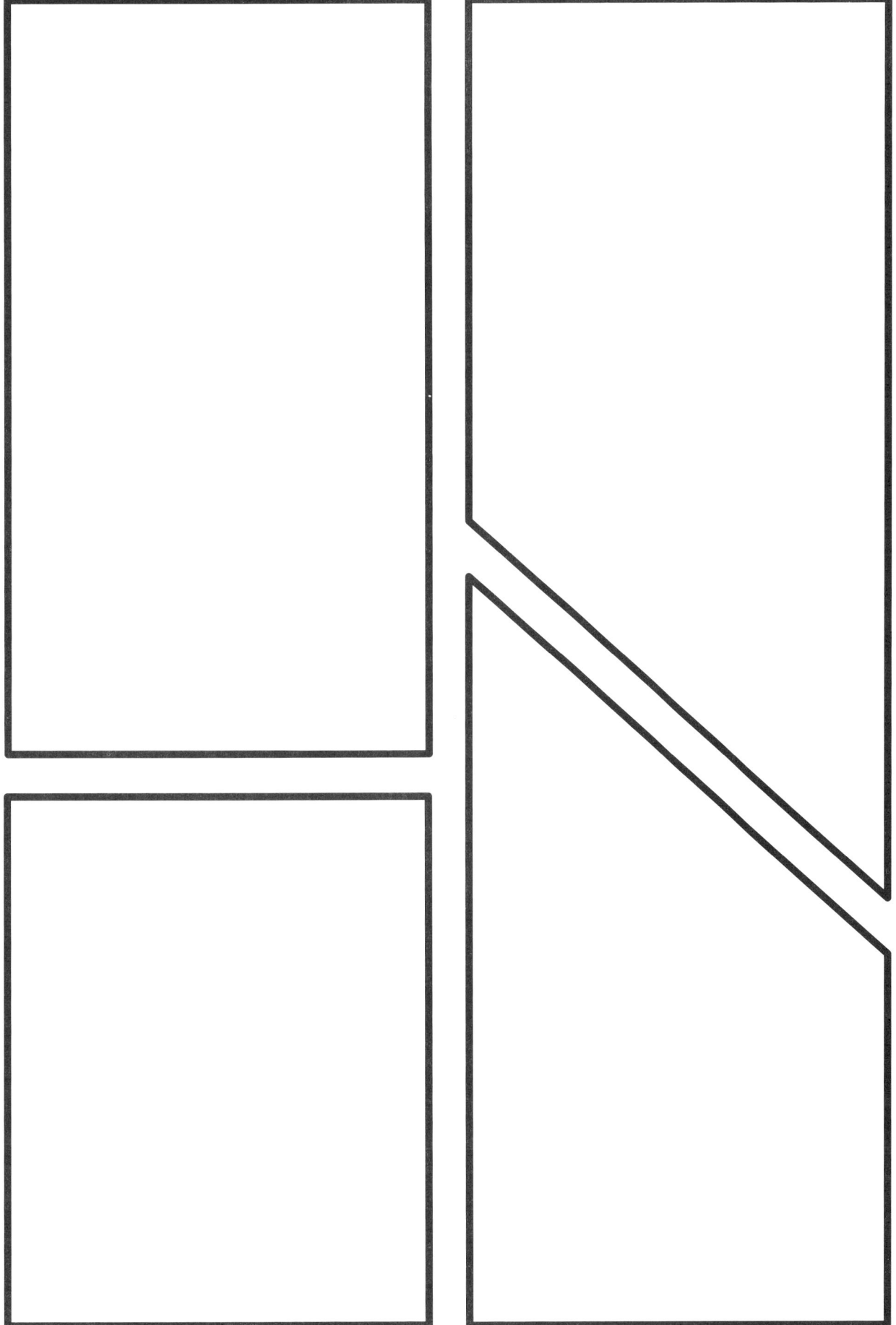

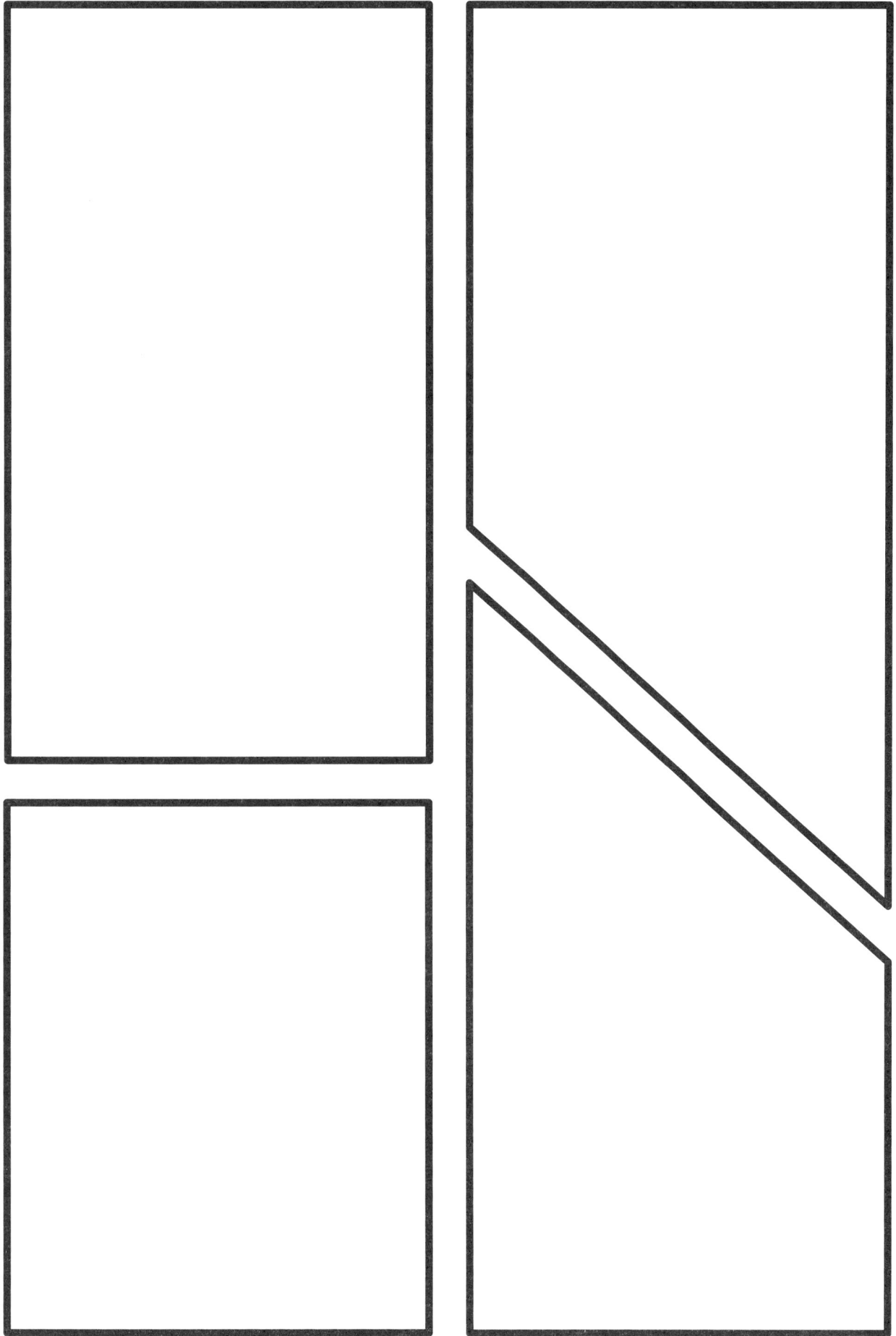

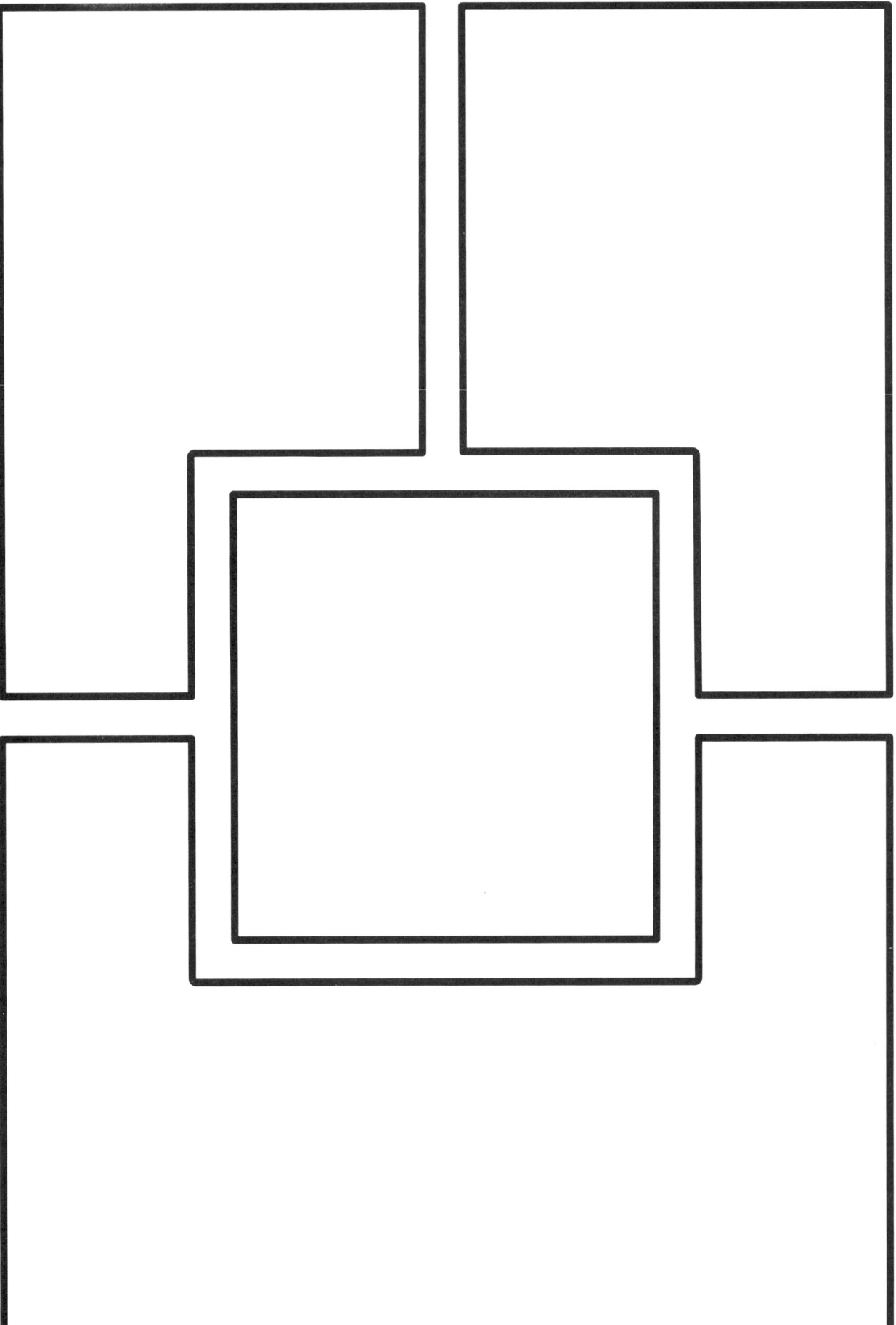

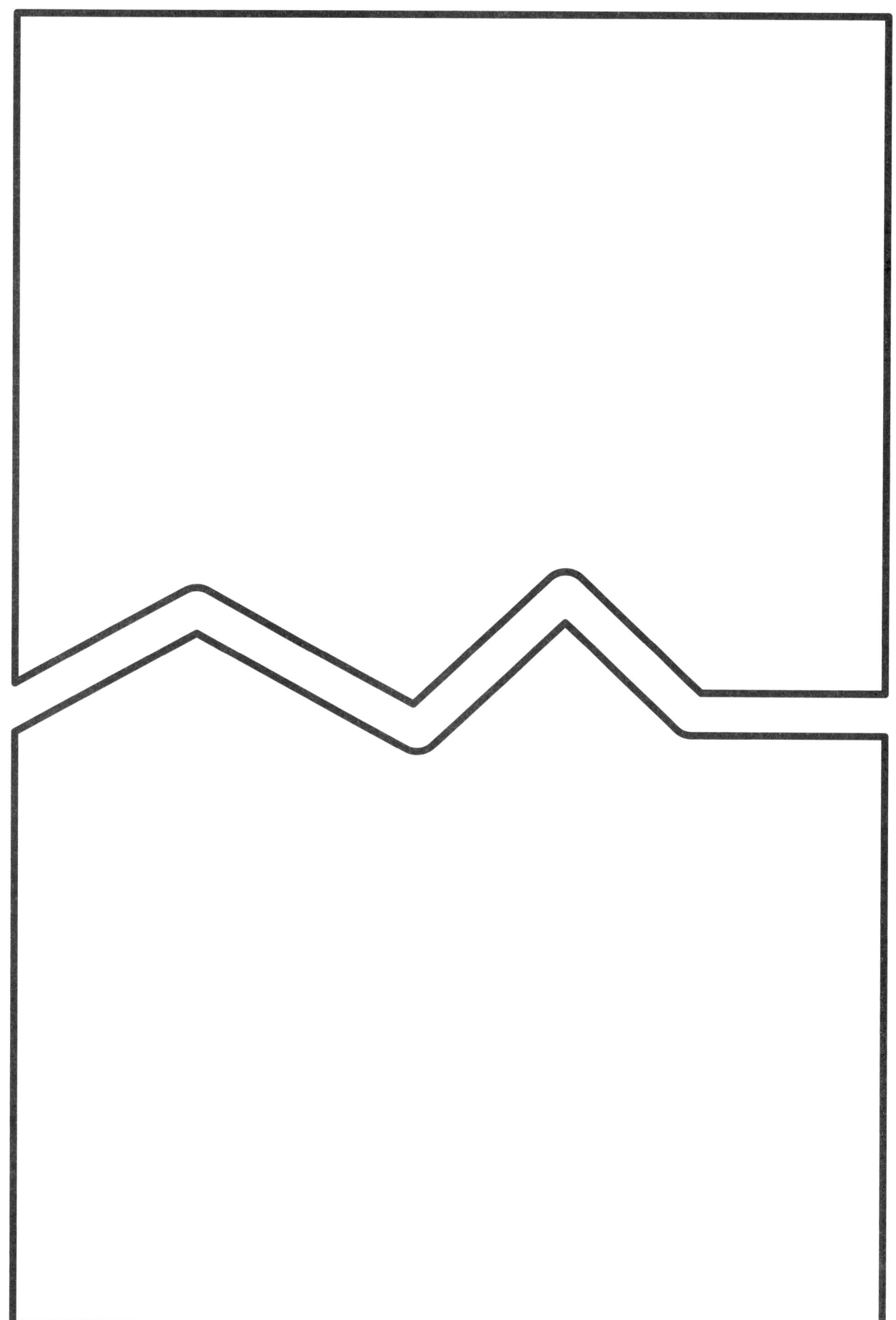

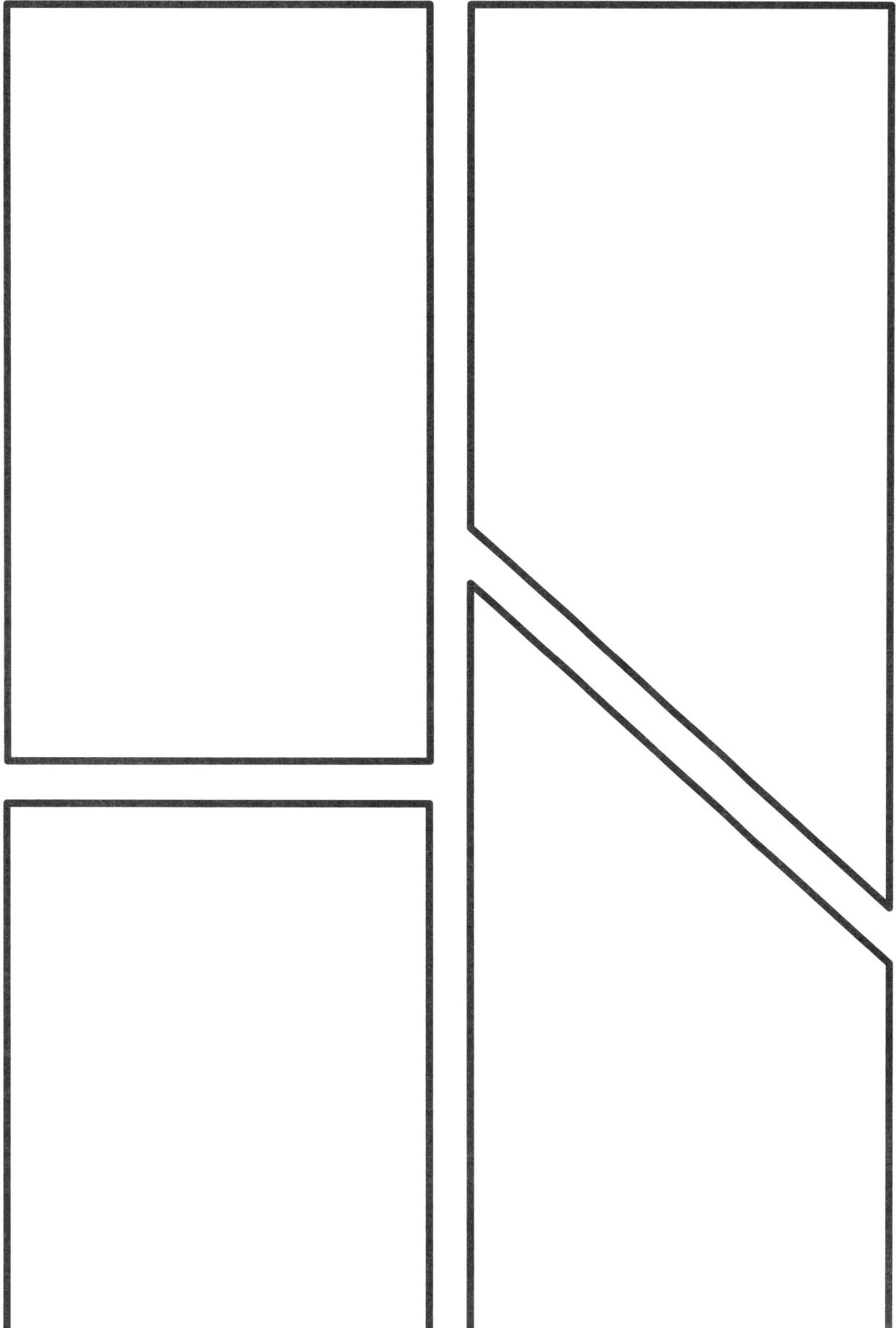

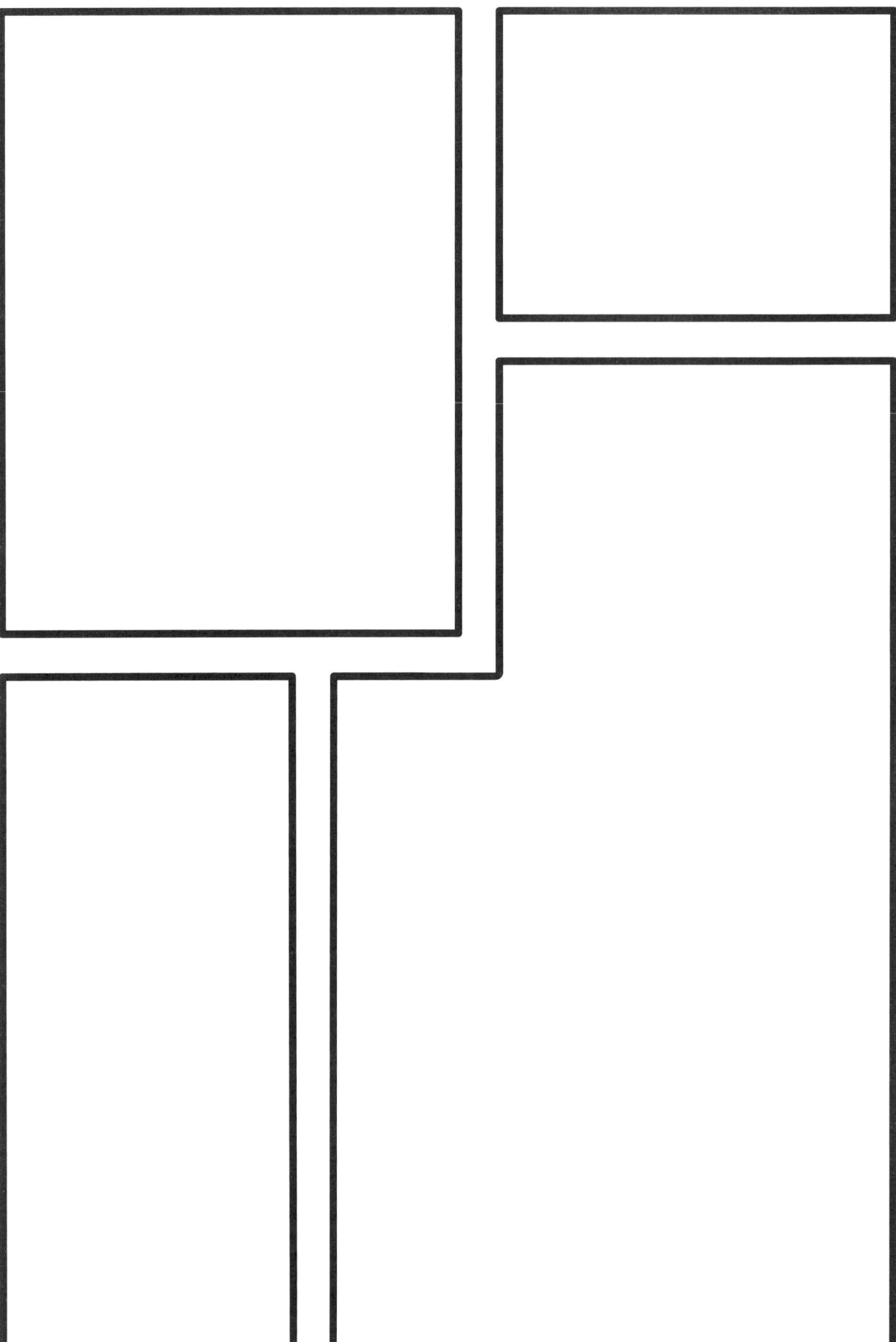

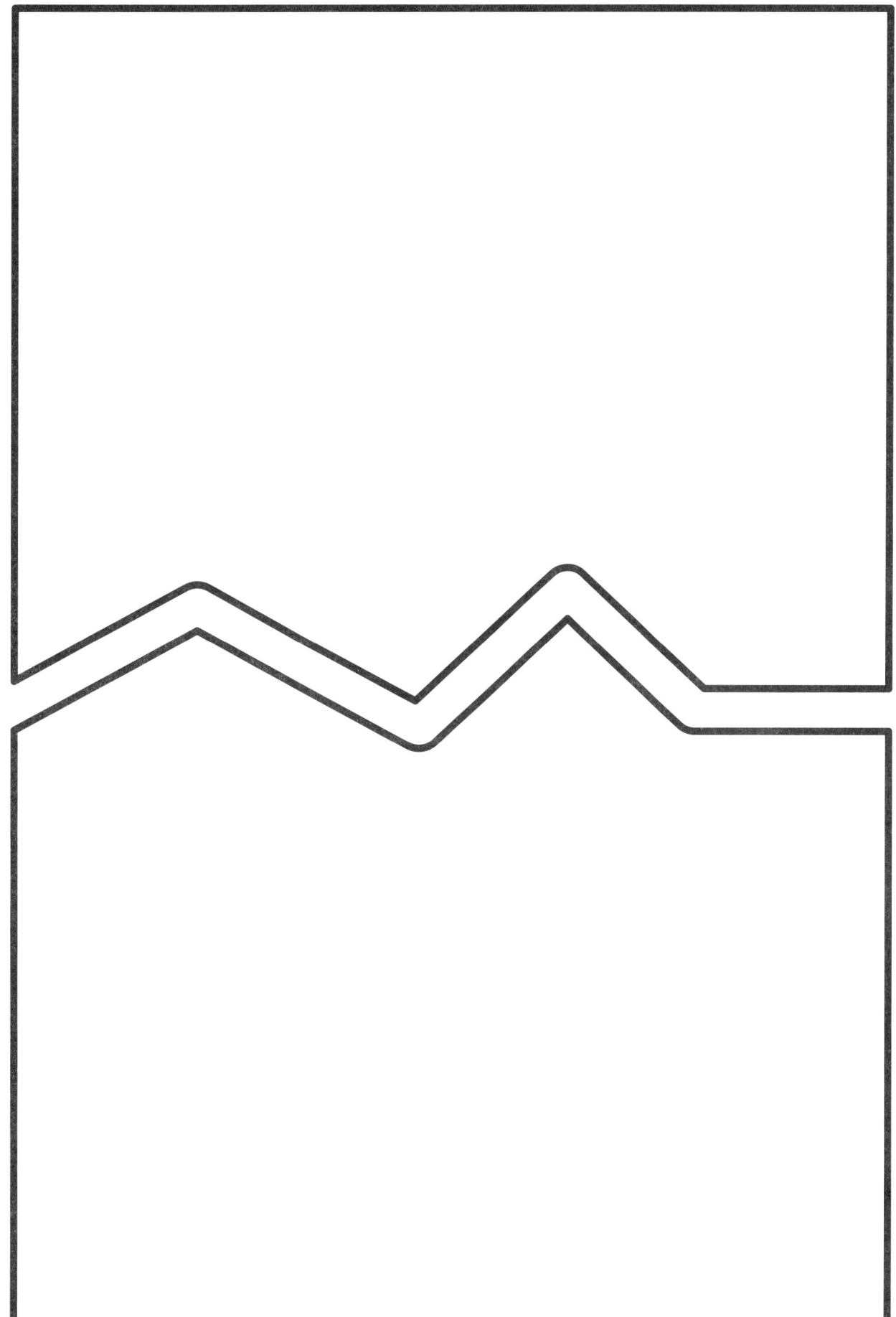

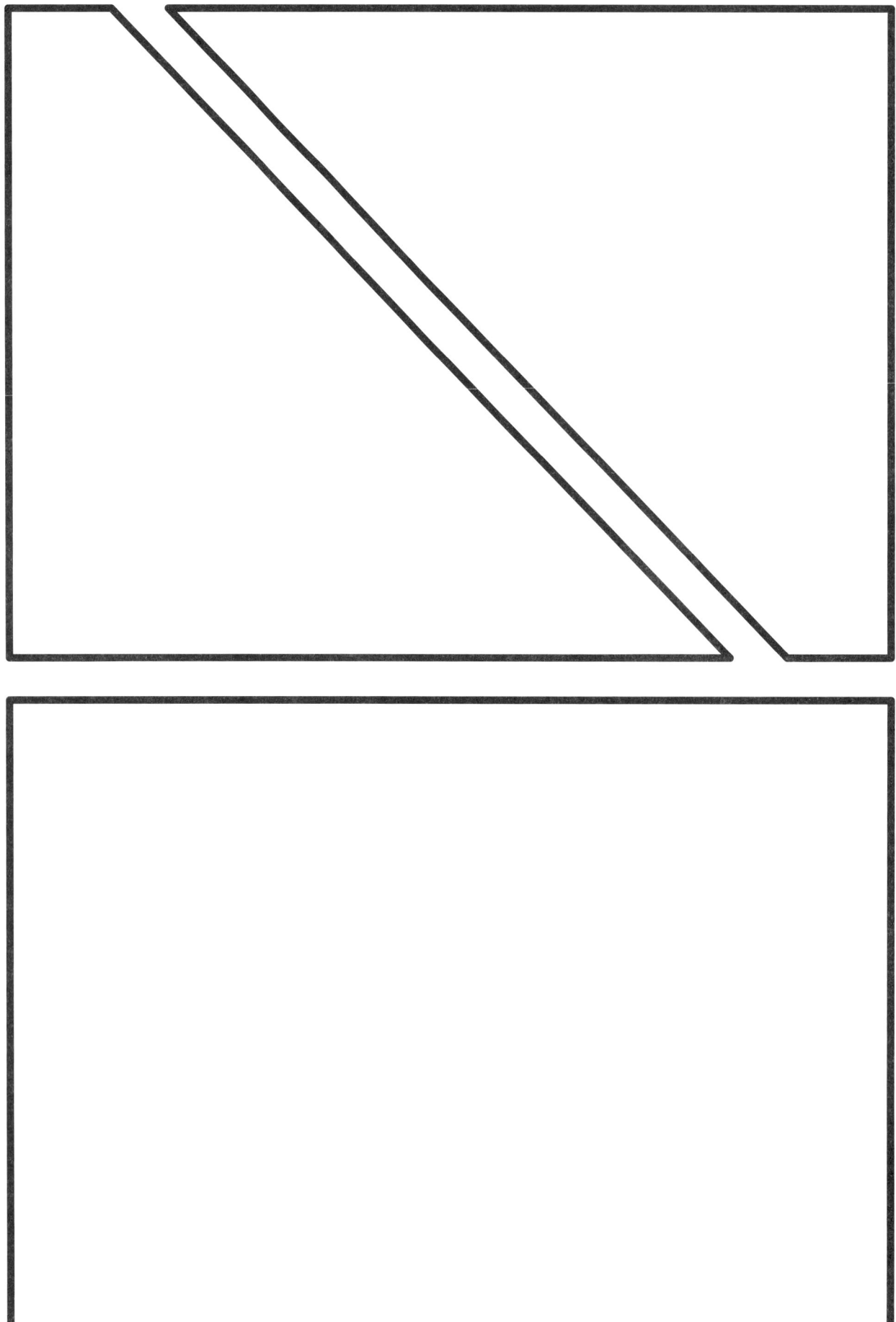

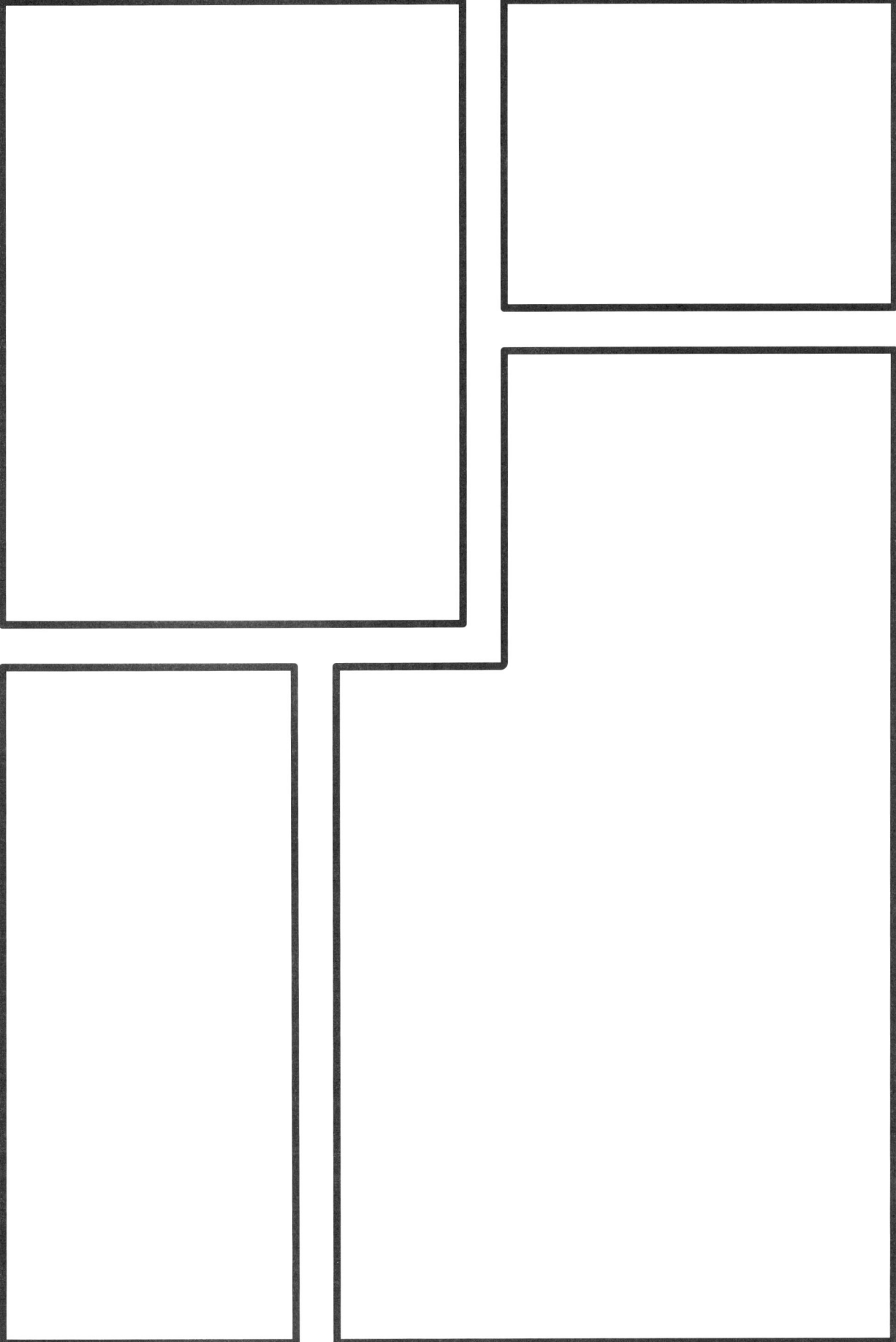

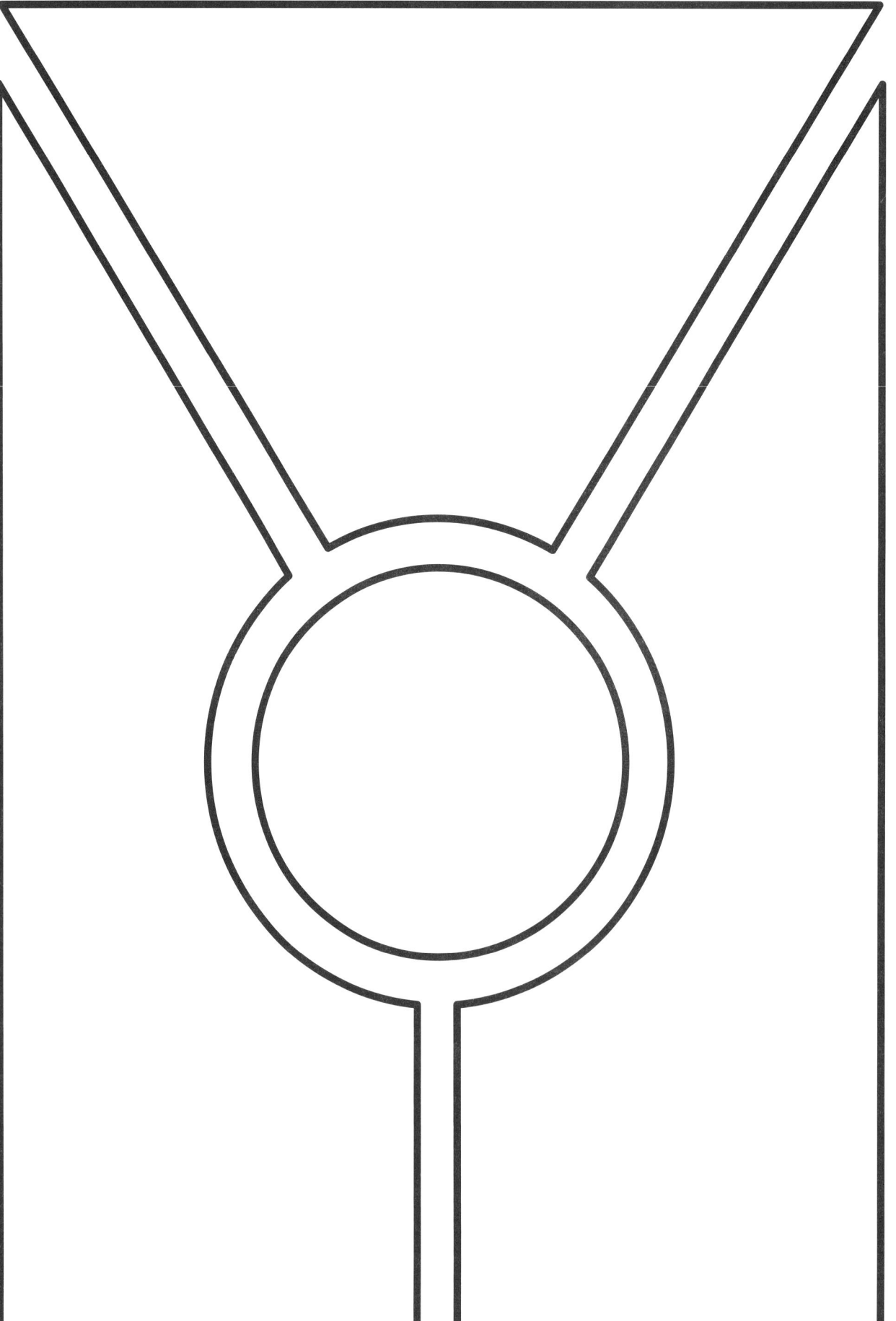

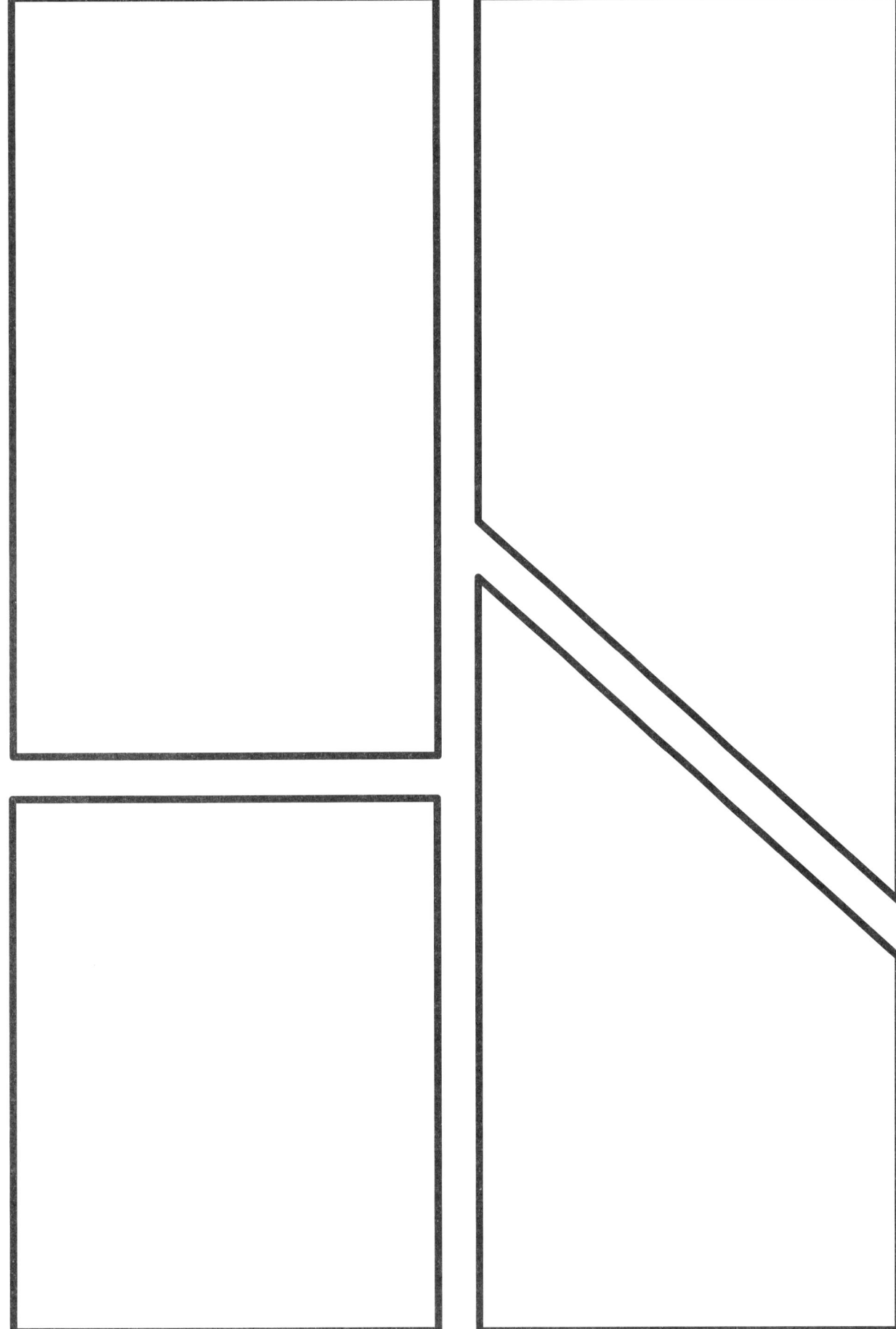

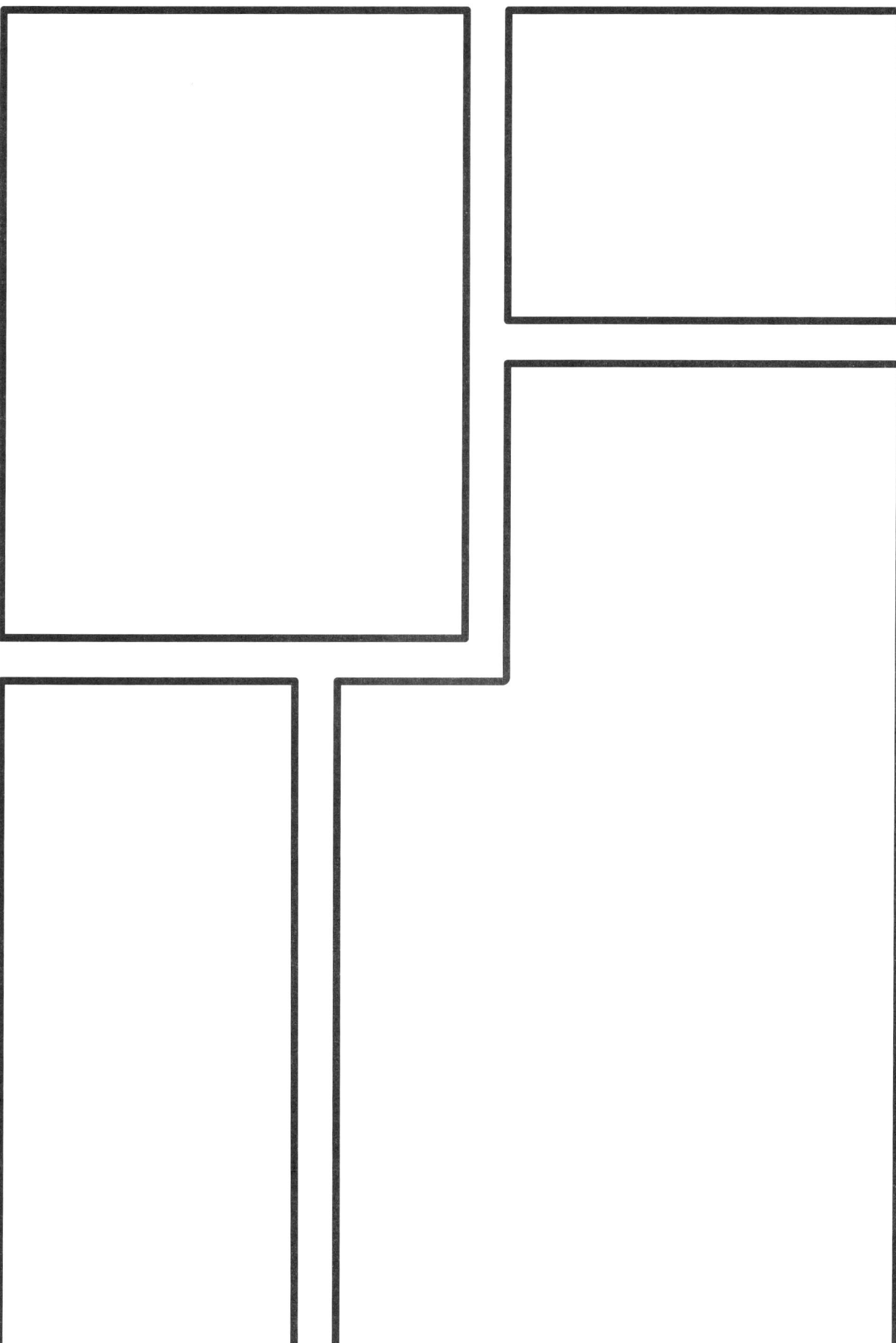

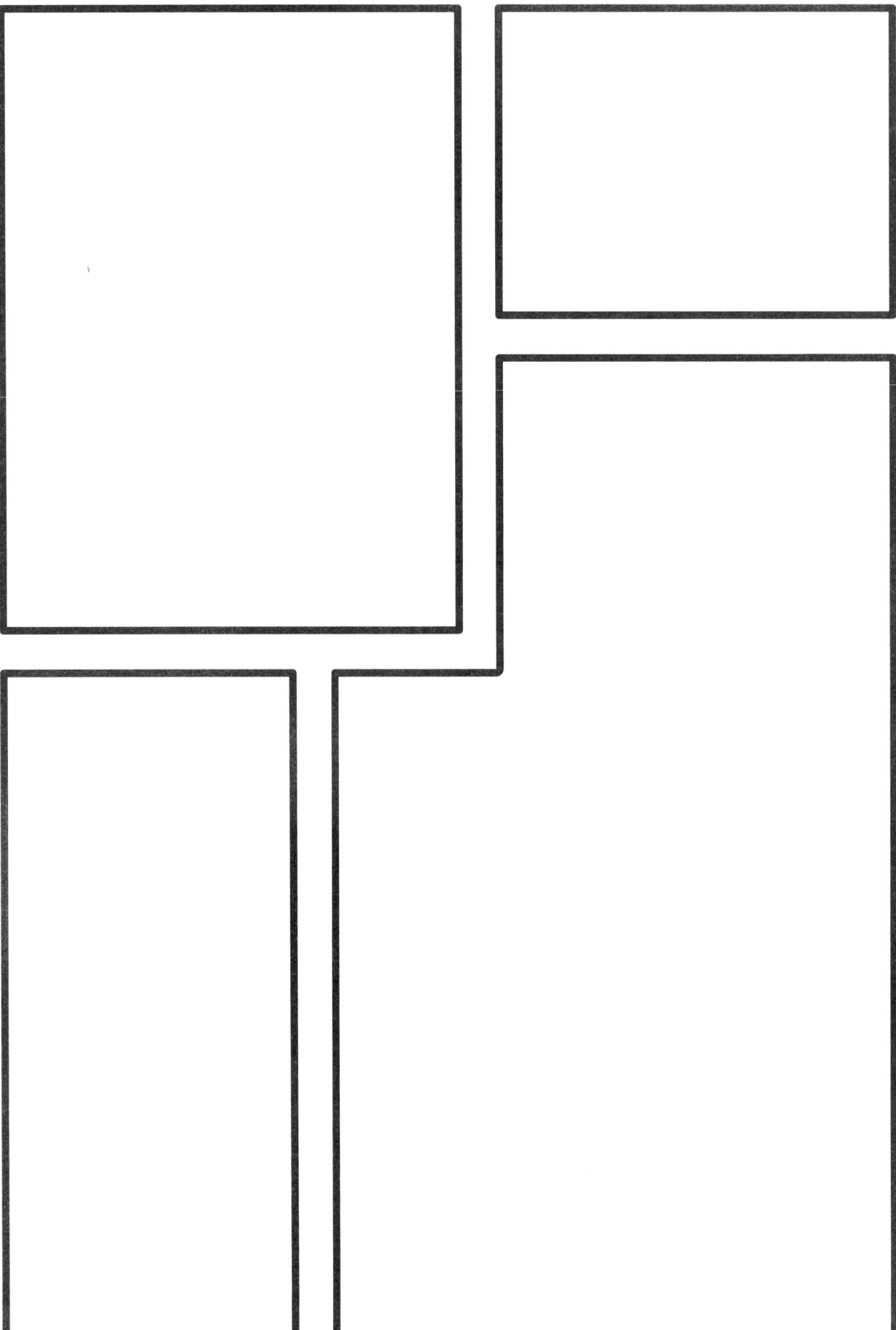

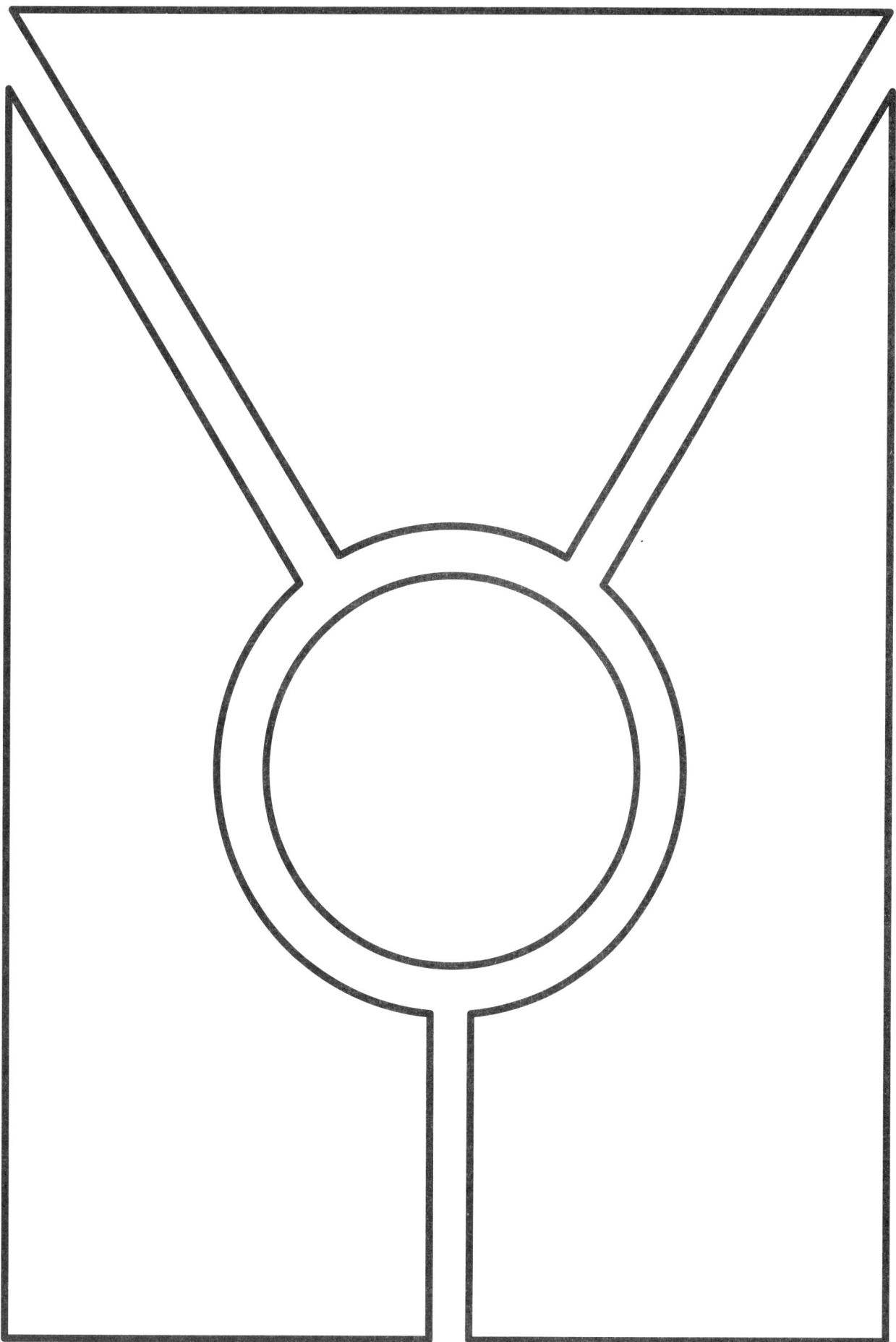

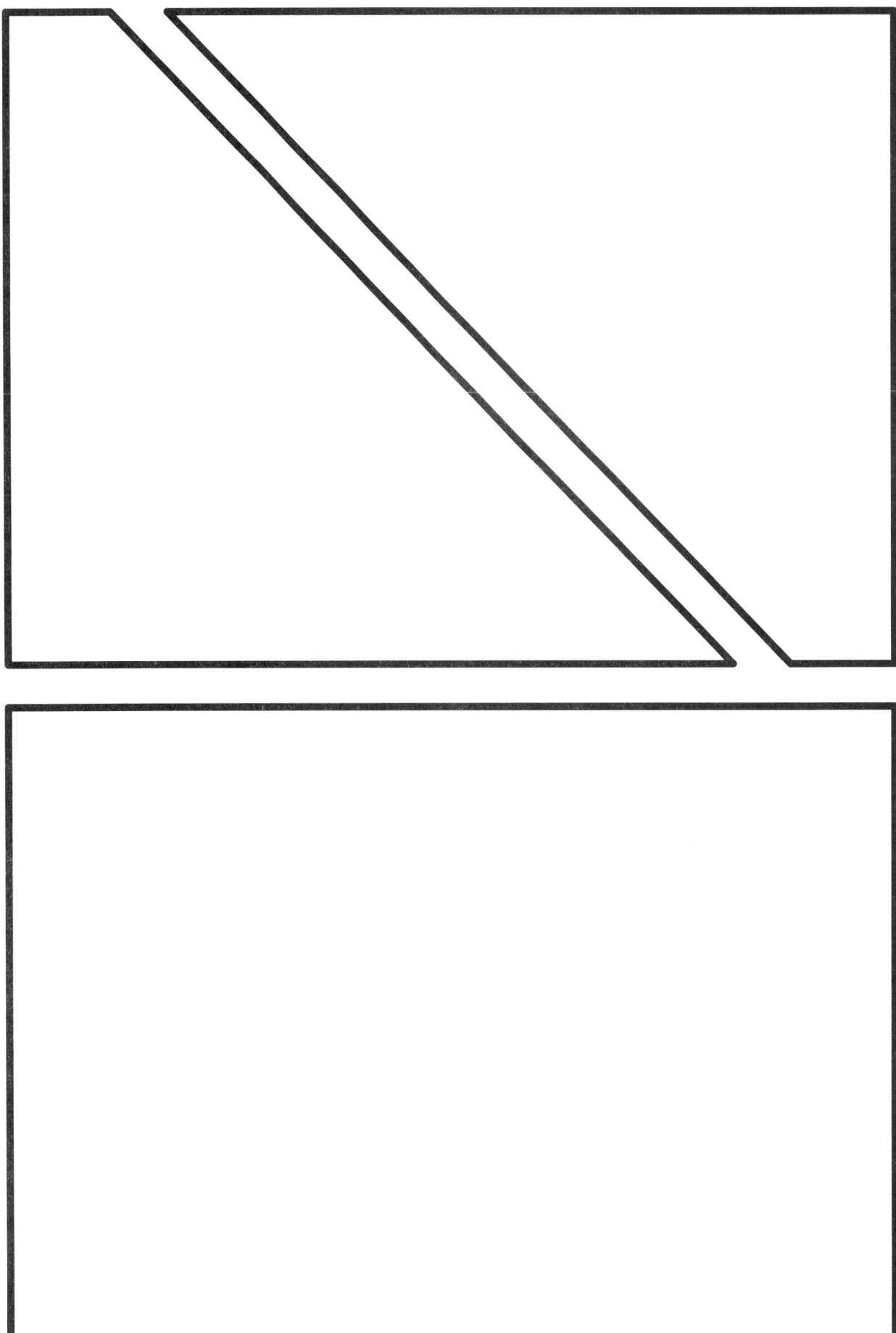

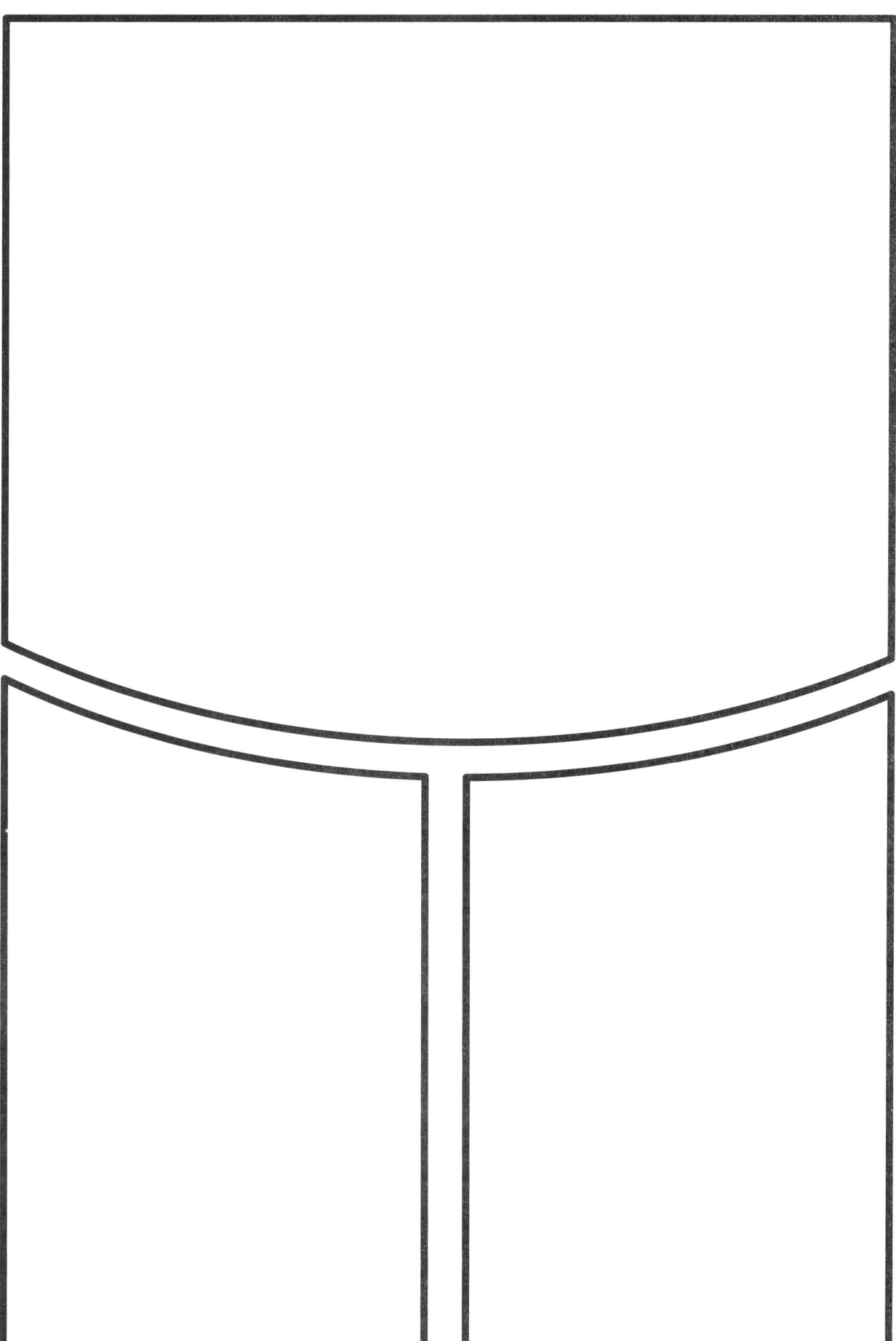

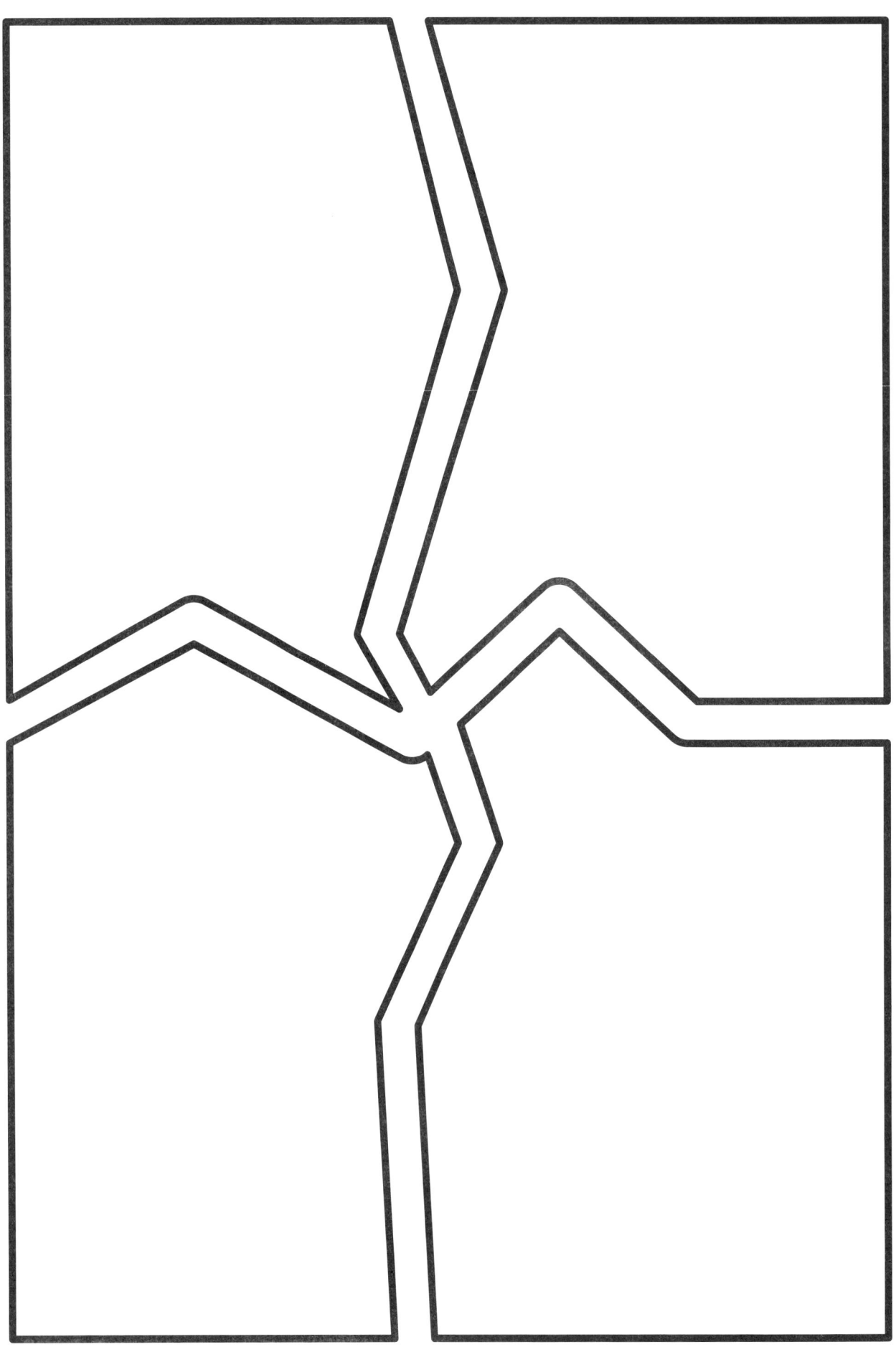

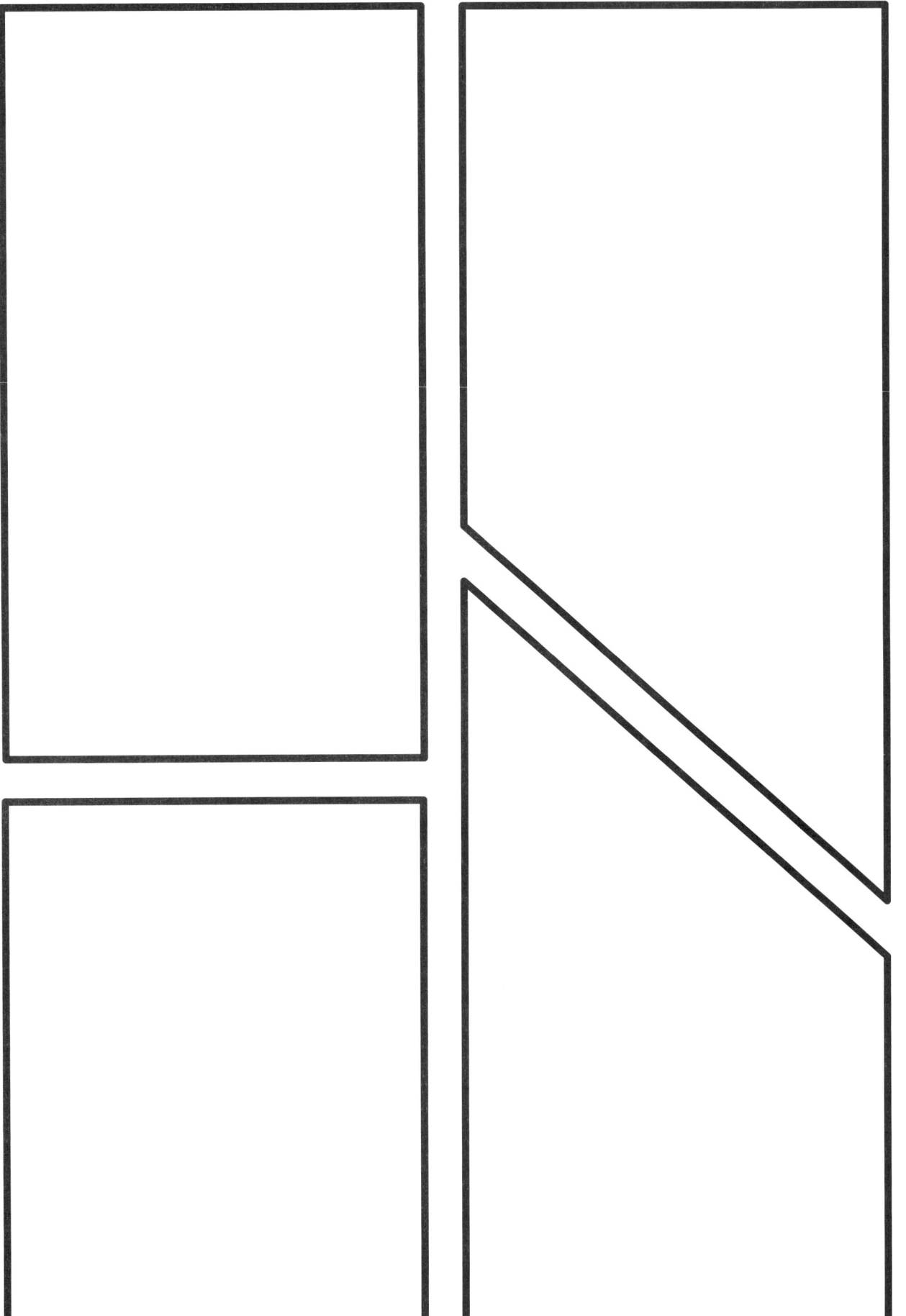

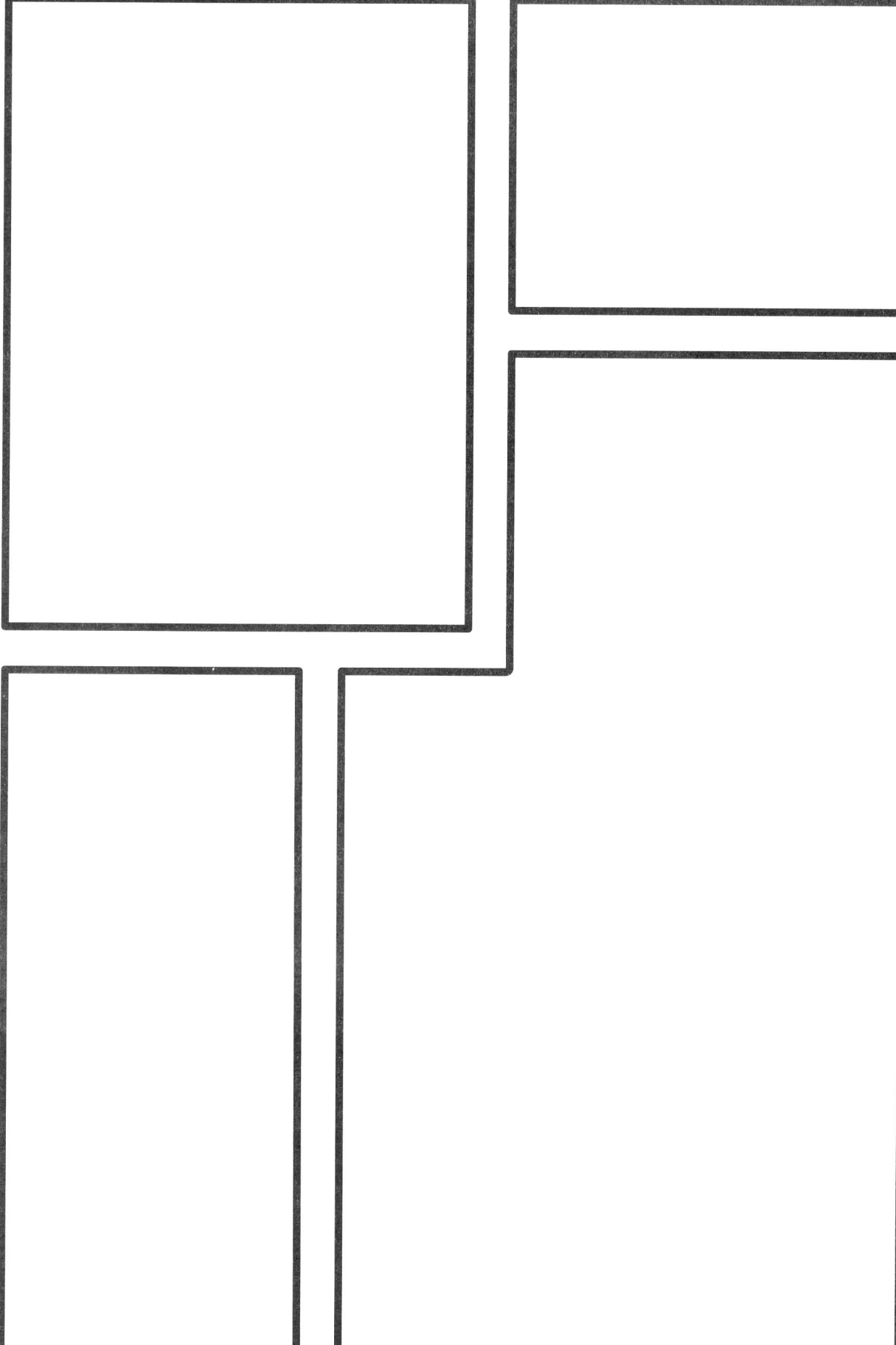